Keturah Revealed

Table of Contents

"Keturah Revealed" is a must have for every library. This book brings the revelation of Abraham's other family that is also apart of the Abrahamic lineage. Dr. Battle's dynamic teaching sheds light on the connection between African and Jewish roots. This teaching will bring healing and deliverance to many cultures and nations!

Dr. Negiel Bigpond
Apostle, Morning Star Church of All Nations
Co-Founder, Two Rivers Native American Training Center

This is an amazing book and a must have for every Kingdom library. Dr. Battle has captured the heart of the Father to bring revelation forward to help restore the African and African American peoples identity to our father Abraham.

Mavel Summers
Honorary Consul of Republic of Honuras
Atlanta, Georgia.

Discovering Your
Jewish Roots

Keturah
Revealed

Dr. Venessa Battle — Series 1
Forward by Rabbi Curt Landry

HERITAGE PUBLISHING

Keturah Revealed

No part of this work may be reproduced or transmitted in any form or by any means, electronic or mechanical, including photocopying and recording, or by any information storage or retrieval system, except as may be expressly permitted by the 1976 Copyright Act or in writing from the publisher. Requests for permission should be addressed to Heritage Publishing, 102 Ivy Hill Lane, Goodlettsville TN, 37072 This book is printed on acid-free paper.

Library of Congress Cataloging-in-Publication Data on file
ISBN 978-0-9815073-2-3

MANUFACTURED IN THE UNITED STATES OF AMERICA

PRAYERS - The most holy place in the world accessible to Jewish people, prayers are offered up at this wall built by King Herod in the first century B.C. Three times a day the Jewish people pray (morning, afternoon, evening) and they do so with phylacteries tied around their forehead and wrist and with white and blue prayer shawls.

Keturah
Revealed

Genesis 25:1
Abraham again took a wife, and her name was Keturah.

African and African-American
Jewish Roots Revealed

Dedication

This book is gratefully dedicated to all the members of Kingdom Culture Ministries, Spiritual Rights Movement & New Gate International Church. Without their love, support, prayers, faithfulness, and commitment I would have never been able to go forth in ministry!

Foreword

"Abraham again took a wife, and her name was Keturah. And she bore him Zimran, Jokshan, Medan, Midian, Ishbak, and Shuah....all these were the children of Keturah.

And Abraham gave all that he had to Isaac. But Abraham gave gifts to the sons of the concubines which Abraham had; and while he was still living he sent them eastward, away from Isaac his son, to the country of the east." -Genesis 25:1-6 (NKJV)

This passage of scripture and this season of our patriarchal father Abraham's life has been overlooked and at times misunderstood. Dr. Venessa Battles writes with anointed insights and brings an extremely revelatory message to readers in a very easily understood way.

Behold, how good and how pleasant it is
For brethren to dwell together in unity!
It is like the precious oil upon the head,
Running down on the beard,
The beard of Aaron,
Running down on the edge of his garments.
It is like the dew of Hermon,
Descending upon the mountains of Zion;
For there the Lord commanded the blessing—
Life forevermore.

-Psalm 133:1-5 (NKJV)
Dr. Venessa Battle's work is revealing regarding the

commanded unity of the brethren. When understanding the ministry of reconciliation we must always go to the root. The root of the wound in Keturah and her sons comes from Abraham and can be healed through Abraham. As a Jewish-Believer, the seed of Abraham, and one who represents Isaac...it is my prayer that you release forgiveness, receive forgiveness, and walk in the commanded blessing of prosperity and unity. This book will help you understand the fatherhood of God and destroy the yoke of the orphan spirit that brings poverty. May God bless you out of Zion as you read and study--in Yeshua's Name!

Rabbi Curt Landry
House of David Ministries

It is said that we receive our identity from our father and nurturing from our mother. Keturah nurtured six sons, so that through them Abraham became "the father of many nations". It is important for many African and African American people to know that your identity comes from Abraham, but it is even more important to know our identity as believers in Jesus Christ is as spiritual children of Abraham, the father of us all. Dr. Battle makes it clear that no matter what our natural lineage is we are now one new man in Christ (Eph 2:15) I strongly endorse Dr. Battle and "Keturah Revealed" This book will give us all deeper revelation of God's plans for our lives and for all the races.

Apostle John Benefiel
Heartland Apostolic Prayer Network

Introduction

It is important that we celebrate God's Highest and Holiest days. He has commanded it and they bring blessings into our lives. Several years ago we began celebrating the Passover, Pentecost, Rosh Shoshanna, and the Ten Days of Awe. As we are learning more about these feasts and Hanukkah, we have begun to walk in the blessings of God as we have never experienced before.

I didn't know where it would lead us, but I knew it was God and we needed to begin somewhere. One of the main things we have had the pleasure of experiencing is His presence in our lives at a greater level.

Through research, studies and information provided by several Jewish rabbis, we have found that the African people have Jewish roots that can be traced all the way back to Abraham, the patriarch of the Israelites. It has been a major year for us as we are coming into our identity and the understanding of who we are in relation to Biblical Studies.

Chapter One

God's Order

As a child growing up in Fort Worth, Texas, our family was one which practiced religion. We went to church and served God in the way we understood. As United Methodists, we were ordered people very big on methods and procedures. I did not know that one day this training would play a major part in my understanding of how God would use these methods and procedures. God is a God that calls His people to operate decently and in order (*1 Cor. 14:40- Let all things be done decently and in order*).

I now understand that God is meticulous in His planning and ordering of things. Many things have happened that prove this. In the creation of mankind, God chose to create man first, and then woman. He then created the birds of the air, the fish of the sea, and all the animals on land with exact precision and order.

Order means "an authoritative direction or instruction; command; mandate; the disposition of things following one after another, as in space or time; succession or sequence; a condition in which each thing is properly disposed with reference to other things and to its purpose; methodical or harmonious arrangement." We are to live in a manner which reflects order.

God has a certain order in which He wants things done. In Exodus the Lord gives Moses decrees and laws in which Israel was to live and serve Him. He sets in place the laws which should be used to govern their lives. The Lord gives them the keys to living a life that will please Him in the Ten Commandments.

The word "exodus" means departure. In God's timing, the exodus of the Israelites from Egypt marked the end of a period of oppression for Abraham's descendants (Genesis 15:13), and the beginning of the fulfillment of the covenant promise to Abraham that his descendants would not only live in the Promised Land, but would also multiply and become a great nation (Genesis 12:1-3,7).

The purpose of the book may be expressed as tracing the rapid growth of Jacob's descendants from Egypt to the establishment of a nation. It deals with the construction of the Ark of the Covenant and the plan for the Tabernacle with its various sacrifices, altars, furniture, ceremonies, and forms of worship.

Exodus 40:4 -"You shall bring in the table and arrange the things that are to be set in order on it; and you shall bring in the lamp stand and light its lamps."

Exodus 40:23 – "and he set the bread in order upon it before the LORD, as the LORD had commanded Moses."

The Book of Leviticus provides instruction and laws to guide a sinful, yet redeemed people in their relationship with a Holy God. There is an emphasis in Leviticus on the need for personal holiness in response to a Holy God. Sin must be atoned for through the offering of proper sacrifices (Chapters 8-10). Other topics covered in the book are diets (clean and unclean foods), childbirth, and diseases which are carefully regulated (Chapters 11-15). In Chapter 16, it describes the Day of Atonement when an annual sacrifice is made for the cumulative sin of the people.

Furthermore, the people of God are to be circumspect in their personal, moral, and social living, in contrast to the then-current practices of the heathen roundabout them (Chapters 17-22).

Certain references in the Book of Leviticus would allow one to believe that God is picky and petty. There are many tiny details, such as offerings have to be presented in certain ways. Sacrificial offerings are so specifically decreed that God even instructs the priests on how animals are to be cut and killed.

Leviticus 1:7 – *"The sons of Aaron the priest shall put fire on the altar, and lay the wood in order on the fire."*

Leviticus 1:8 – *"Then the priests, Aaron's sons, shall lay the parts, the head, and the fat in order on the wood that is on the fire upon the altar."*

Leviticus 1:12 – *"And he shall cut it into its pieces, with its head and its fat; and the priest shall lay them in order on the wood that is on the fire upon the altar."*

As you begin to read and study Leviticus 2, God lists the unclean and the clean animals. This list is so detailed that it could cause your head to spin. As God gives instructions about the dress and behavior of the priests, He is no less thorough in His instruction. God emphasizes order at the beginning of Leviticus; and deals with more than a million people who had lived under the chains of slavery for 400 years; this required great order. Every person in the Israelite's camp could not become a law unto themselves. Lawlessness leads to chaos and chaos to destruction and so God placed order at the top of His priority list as He sought to guide His slave children from bondage to freedom.

Leviticus 24:8 - *"Every Sabbath he shall set it in order before the LORD continually, being taken from the children of Israel by an everlasting covenant."*

The Book of Numbers is universal and timeless. It reminds believers of the spiritual warfare in which they are engaged. Numbers is the book of the service and the walk of God's people.

The Book of Numbers essentially bridges the gap between the Israelites receiving the Law (Exodus and Leviticus) and preparing them to enter the Promised Land (Deuteronomy and Joshua).

Numbers 10:28 – *"Thus was the order of the march of children of Israel, according to their armies, when they began their journey."*

The Book of Deuteronomy was given to remind them of

> *"Be strong and courageous, because you will lead these people to inherit the land I swore to their forefathers to give them. Be strong and very courageous. Be careful to obey all the laws my servant Moses gave you; do not turn from it to the right or to the left, that you may be successful wherever you go.*

God's law and God's power. The book gives instruction to a new generation of Israelites who were about to enter a new land with many dangers and temptations. The Israelites are commanded to remember four things: God's faithfulness, God's holiness, God's blessings, and God's warnings. The first three chapters recap the trip from Egypt to their current location, Moab. Chapter 4 is a call to obedience, to be faithful to the God Who was faithful to them. Chapters 5 through 26 are a repetition of the law, and The Ten Commandments, the laws concerning sacrifices and special days and the rest of the laws given to the new generation.

"Blessings are promised to those who obey (Deuteronomy 5:29; 6:17-19; 11:13-15), and famine is promised to those who

break the law (Deuteronomy 11:16-17)."

The theme of blessing and cursing is continued in Chapters 27-30. This portion of the book ends with a clear choice set before Israel: *"I have set before you life and death blessing and cursing."* God's desire for His people is found in what He commands: *"choose life" (Deuteronomy 30:19).*

Deuteronomy 17:10 - *"You shall do according to the sentence which they pronounce upon you in that place which the LORD chooses. And you shall be careful to do according to all that they order you."*

The Book of Joshua provides an overview of the military campaigns to conquer the land area that God had promised. Following the exodus from Egypt and the subsequent 40 years of the wilderness wanderings, the newly-formed nation is now poised to enter the Promised Land, conquer the inhabitants, and occupy the territory. The overview that we have here gives abbreviated and selective details of many of the battles and the manner in which the land was not only conquered, but how it was divided into tribal areas. Here the Lord gives Joshua marching orders.

Joshua 1:6-9 - *"Be strong and courageous, because you will lead these people to inherit the land I swore to their forefathers to give them. Be strong and very courageous. Be careful to obey all the laws my servant Moses gave you; do not turn from it to the right or to the left, that you may be successful wherever you go. Do not let this Book of the Law depart from your mouth; meditate on it day and night, so that you may be careful to do everything written in it. Then you will be prosperous and successful. Have I not commanded you? Be strong and courageous. Do not be terrified; do not be discouraged, for the LORD your God will be with wherever you go."*

The Book of Joshua continues the story of the Israelites after the exodus from Egypt. The book chronicles the approximately 20 years of Joshua's leadership of the people after Moses anointed him at the end of Deuteronomy. The 24 chapter divisions of the Book of Joshua can be summarized as follows:

- Chapters 1-12: Entering and conquering the Promised Land.
- Chapters 13-22: Instructions for distributing the portions of the Promised Land.
- Chapters 23-24: Joshua's farewell address.

Joshua leaves the children of Israel with the order of success.

Joshua 24:14-15 - *"Now fear the LORD and serve him with all faithfulness. Throw away the gods your forefathers worshiped beyond the River and in Egypt, and serve the LORD. But if serving the LORD seems undesirable to you, then choose for yourselves this day whom you will serve, whether the gods your forefathers served beyond the River, or the gods of the Amorites, in whose land you are living. But as for me and my household, we will serve the LORD."*

In these five books of the Bible we see the order of God:

1. He delivers Israel first out of bondage and starts them on a road to progression in order to fulfill the promises spoken to Abraham.

2. He begins to establish them as a nation and gives them instructions on how this would be accomplished.

3. He tells them how to worship and gives the plan for the Tabernacle with its various sacrifices, altars, furniture, ceremonies, and forms of worship.

4. He gives them His laws and teaches them how to live a holy life.

5. He begins preparing them for warfare and explains the need to go in and possess the land and territory.

6. He positions the next generation for His move.

7. He sends them into the Promised Land to conquer and occupy the territory.

God's order is impeccable! He couldn't begin to position them to go into the Promised Land until they were first delivered. He couldn't begin to establish them as a nation until they were first delivered. He couldn't teach them how to live holy until they understood His way of worship. He couldn't allow them to go into the promise without first preparing them for warfare.

Thus, we can see that God's order is important. Today, many people in the body of Christ try to go forward with the things God has called them to do without following His order. It causes people to become discouraged, disappointed, and disheartened. Many people are well ahead of God's plans for their life because they have done things out of God's order.

We have become a generation that lacks order and discipline in all areas in the kingdom of God. God has a profound quality of order. We don't usually recognize this fact and its importance.

I didn't recognize this fact and its importance until I went to the Hebrew definition of "order," which has many meanings. In the context of this book, with God's Levitical instructions, I would like to focus on a word used in Hebrew to describe "order." It is the word "frame."

In Psalm 119:133, it says, *"Order my steps in Thy word: and let not any iniquity have dominion over me."* In other words, David asks God to "frame" his steps, so that nothing unrighteous will rule or dominate or be given power over him. The "order" or "framing" of David's life by God protects him from evil.

Isaiah 9:7 – *"Of the increase of His government and peace, there will be no end. Upon the throne of David and over His kingdom, to order it and establish it with judgment and justice from that time forward, even forever. The zeal of the LORD of hosts will perform this."*

With this being said, we must understand God's order and His ways of doing things. We must get an understanding of God's order for this end time move of God to usher in the King!

Deuteronomy 8:6 – *"Therefore you shall keep the commandments of the LORD your God, to walk in His ways and to fear Him."*

In this book we will explore how God ordered Abraham the Patriarch's steps so that he would have sons which will go all over the earth and bless all families in the earth.

Chapter Two

Where Did It All Begin

I n order to get a better understanding of our father Abraham, we should go back to Genesis 11:27. This is the genealogy of Terah: Terah begot Abram, Nahor, and Haran. Haran begot Lot.

28) And Haran died before his father Terah in his native land, in Ur of the Chaldeans.
29) Then Abram and Nahor took wives: the name of Abram's wife was Sarai, and the name of Nahor's wife, Milcah, the daughter of Haran the father of Milcah and the father of Iscah.
30) But Sarai was barren; she had no child.
31) And Terah took his son Abram and his grandson Lot, the son of Haran, and his daughter-in-law Sarai, his son Abram's wife, and they went out with the Chaldeans to go to the land of Canaan; and they came to Haran and dwelt there.
32) So the days of Terah were two hundred and five years, and Terah died in Haran.

Terah was the father Haran, Nahor, and Abraham, and with another wife, also the father of Sarah (Abraham married his half-sister Sarah, i.e. Genesis 20:12). Terah first settled in Ur Of The Chaldees, where his son Haran, the father of Lot, died. Terah then migrated with Abraham and Lot, together with their families, from Ur, at first apparently intending to accompany them to Canaan, but he stopped at Haran where he remained for the rest of his long life. Terah was an idol worshipper), a family religion that righteous Abraham did not continue.

"Long ago your forefathers, including Terah the father of Abraham and Nahor, lived beyond the River and worshiped other gods"

Abraham was a semi-nomadic shepherd to whom God revealed himself, made promises, and entered into covenant concerning Abraham's offspring and the land that they would inherit in the future. Abraham's belief in these promises was counted by God as righteousness and his faith shaped his life. Ultimately these promises find their fulfillment in Jesus the Messiah and all those who trust in Yahweh, the true God, Abraham's spiritual children.

Abraham was called both a Hebrew (14:13) and an Aramean (Deuteronomy 26:5; cf.25:20; 28:5; 31:20, 24). He was born in Ur and moved to Haran with his father Terah.

At God's call, he traveled to Canaan and lived for a while in various localities, in particular Shechem, Hebron, Bethel, and the Negev desert, with sojourns to Egypt and Gerar. Genesis records that he led a band of armed men to rescue his nephew Lot from kings who had captured him, interceded for Sodom and Gomorrah (Lot's wicked residence), paid tithes to the Melchizedek, king of (Jeru) Salem, and entertained angels.

The story we usually hear is he bore a son, Ishmael, by his wife's servant who became the father of the Arab nations. In Biblical times, the changing of one's name was significant and used to symbolize the binding of a covenant. In this case, God promised to put an end to her barrenness and give her a child (Isaac).

His heir Isaac was born to Abraham and Sarah in their old age supernaturally by God. His devotion to God was such that he was willing to sacrifice his only son. He grew wealthy, married again after Sarah's death, and died at the age of 175 years. I think that we should look again, because in Genesis 25:1-6, there is a part of his life that seemed hidden. Abraham had another wife, named Keturah who was an Ethiopian (a black woman) who is rarely mentioned. In this book, we will talk about the members of this part of Abraham's family.

Abraham's ancestors were idolaters and polytheists (worshippers of many gods). Joshua reminded the people, *"Long ago your forefathers, including Terah the father of Abraham and Nahor, lived beyond the River and worshiped other gods"* (Joshua 24:2). Jacob's wife Rachel, who probably grew up with Terah's religion, stole her father's "household gods." (Joshua 3:32-35; 35:2-4).

Archaeology shows that both Ur in Lower Mesopotamia and Haran in Upper Mesopotamia were centers of moon worship. Even the names Terah, Laban, Sarah, and Milcah contain elements that reveal allegiance to the moon-god.

Sumerian culture in southern Mesopotamia had a number of

gods in its pantheon: four leading dieties—An, Enlil, Enki, and Ninhursag—and three chief astral deities—Nanna (the moon), Nanna's son Utu (the sun), and Nanna's daughter Inanna. Enlil was considered the chief god with his cult center at the city of Nippur.

Other Sumerian cities had their own special deities as well. Nanna, the moon-god, was the main deity of the Sumerian city of Ur, later known by its Semitic name, Sin. This male deity was also known in the north from several inscriptions to "sin/Shahar, the Lord of Haran" [4] and was the tutelary god of Haran. The moon-god's symbol was the crescent moon and worship in Sumer involved temples as well as ziggurats with small temples on the top. These temples were staffed by priests (who offered sacrifices and made libations), singers and musicians, as well as male and female prostitutes (whose activities many scholars relate to the fertility cult). Much later than Abraham, the Israelites are warned against worship of the moon, sun, and stars (Deuteronomy 4:19; 17:2-5), though this kind of worship continued under idolatrous kings (2 Kings 23:5-12).

There is Only One God

Genesis 12:1 – *"Now the LORD had said to Abram: 'Get out of your country, from your family and from your father's house, to a land that I will show you.'"*

Abraham's faith grew as God revealed himself. By the time we see him Genesis 12 he is a monotheist, a worshipper of one God. He apparently used two words for God—"El," the generic Canaanite name for the cosmic deity and "Yahweh." Yahweh is sometimes translated "Jehovah" in various versions of the Bible, including the King James Version (KJV), New International Version (NIV), Revised Standard Version (RSV), New Revised

Standard Version (NRSV) and others, following the Jewish tradition of not pronouncing the divine name, but substituting "Adonai" for "Lord" instead. Abraham called this God by several other names compounded with Yahweh and El:

God Most High (El Elyon, 14:19, 22, "maker of heaven and earth")

Almighty God (El Shaddai, 17:1)

Everlasting/eternal God (El Olam, 21:33- "Yahweh")

Jehovah-Jireh (22:14, "the Lord the Provider")

Abraham's monotheism contrasts sharply with the polytheism of his forefathers (Joshua 24:2). He believed God to be the Lord of the cosmos (14:22; 24:3), supreme judge of mankind (15:14; 18:25), controller of nature (18:14; 19:24, 20:17), highly exalted (14:22) and eternal (21:33).

Whenever God spoke to him, he obeyed immediately in faith. Abraham's relationship with God was personal rather than formal.

However, Abraham and the other patriarchs practiced various forms of worship, including building altars, offering sacrifices, calling on the name of Yahweh, circumcision, prayer, making vows, and tithing—as well as planting trees and setting up monuments. We'll examine these further as we study the details of Abraham's life.

Abram was Called by God

God told Abram to leave his native land and his father's house for a land that God would show him, promising to make of him a great nation, bless him, make his name great, bless those who blessed him, and curse those who cursed him.

Genesis 12:1-3

1) "Now the LORD had said to Abram: "Get out of your

*country, from your family and from your father's house, to a
land that I will show you.*

*2) "I will make you a great nation; I will bless you, And
make your name great; And you shall be a blessing.*

*3) "I will bless those who bless you, And I will curse him
who curses you; And in you all the families of the earth shall be
blessed."*

Following God's command, at age 75, Abram took his wife
Sarai, his nephew Lot, and the wealth and persons that they had
acquired in Haran, and traveled to the terebinth of Moreh at
Shechem in Canaan.
Genesis 12:4-6:

*4) "So Abram departed as the LORD had spoken to him,
and Lot went with him. And Abram was seventy-five years old
when he departed from Haran.*

*5) "Then Abram took Sarai his wife and Lot his brother's
son, and all their possessions that they had gathered, and the
people whom they had acquired in Haran, and they departed to
go to the land of Canaan. So they came to the land of Canaan.*

*6) "Abram passed through the land to the place of
Shechem, as far as the terebinth tree of Moreh. And the
Canaanites were then in the land."*

God appeared to Abram to tell him that God would assign
the land to his heirs, and Abram built an altar to God. Abram
then moved to the hill country east of Bethel and built an altar
to God there and invoked God by name (Genesis 12:8). Then
Abram journeyed toward the Negev. (Genesis 12:7-9).

*7) "Then the LORD appeared to Abram and said, 'To your
descendants I will give this land.' And there he built an altar to
the LORD, who had appeared to him.*

8) "And he moved from there to the mountain east of Bethel, and he pitched his tent with Bethel on the west and AI on the east; there he built an altar to the LORD and called on the name of the LORD.

9) "So Abram journeyed, going on still toward the South, Abram and Sarai."

The land of Canaan was devastated by a severe famine, so

> *"shall be a wild donkey of a man, his hand against everyone and everyone's hand against him, and he shall dwell over against all his kinsmen."*

Abram and Lot and their households travelled south to northern Egypt. The biblical matriarch Sarah was the wife of Abraham and the mother of Isaac. Information about Sarah comes from Genesis. Chapters 11-23.

The Hebrew name Sarah indicates a woman of high rank and is sometimes translated as "princess." It also means "lady." Sarah was about ten years younger than her half-brothers Abraham (they had the sane father, but different mothers, see Genesis 20:12).

They were married before they left Ur, located in what

is today southern Iraq (Abraham and Sarah were in Iraq, an incredible irony considering the state of Middle East tensions today) for a journey, under The Lord's guidance, to a new land that would become the focus of God's plan of salvation for all of humanity (Genesis 11:29-31).

Abraham and Sarah lived and were married in Haran. When Abraham was 75 years old, God commanded him to leave his home, and Sarah followed her husband to Canaan. Sarah, the wife of Abraham, was very beautiful. Her beauty caused trouble for Abraham (Genesis 12, Genesis 20).The first incident prominently reveals a 65-year-old Sarah journeying to Egypt with Abraham during a period of famine in Canaan.

Despite her age, Sarah was beautiful and Abraham was afraid that if the Pharaoh found out that Sarah was his wife, he would kill him and take her. Sarah agreed with her husband to lie about her real relationship with him. He pretended that Sarah was his sister, and the Pharaoh did take her, giving Abraham many material possessions in exchange. God then sent plagues to punish the house of Pharaoh until he released her and sent Abraham on his way.

A similar incident transpired later in the Bible with King Abimelech of Gerar. He also took Sarah, thinking she was Abraham's sister. God told him the truth in a dream.

Abimelech returned Sarah to Abraham, along with a present of animals, slave, gold and silver.
All the promises in the Scriptures are given to man and women alike. God loves His children and He will protect us.

You too are a daughter of Abraham. Discover the promises of God in the Scriptures and claim them by faith. There was nothing special about Sarah and Abraham, they both had issues, but Abraham lied about his wife and convinced her to agree with him exposing her to the risk of being raped.

God Himself protected Sarah, supernaturally on two separate occasions from being defiled. Who said God treats women as second class citizens?

Women, you may have an unreliable husband who exposes you to danger or unnecessary stress, but don't be bitter against him. Your protection comes from God's promises. Pray that God will touch your husband's heart. Sarah made Abraham into the man of God that we all know him to be today. She played her part in God's plan for the human race.

The first piece of information the Bible gives about Sarah is that she was barren. This was significant since God promised Abraham earlier that his children would become a great nation. Sarah was a compassionate woman. She had no children, and erroneously thought it was her fault. She asked Abraham to have a child through their servant Hagar (Genesis 16).

After 10 years of living in Canaan, when Sarah still had not conceived, she gave Abraham her maid Hagar as a concubine. Once Hagar conceived, Hagar lowered her opinion of Sarah, and Sarah began to treat her harshly. Hagar ran away and returned only after God spoke to her, blessed her and ordered her to go back to Sarah. When Abraham was 86 years old, Hagar gave birth to Ishmael.

Abram and Sarai were trying to make sense of how he would become a progenitor of nations since it had already been 10 years of living in Canaan, and still no child had been born from Abram's seed. Sarai then offered her Egyptian servant, Hagar, for Abram to consort with her so that she might have a child by her, in a sense. Abram consented and had intercourse with Hagar.

The result of these actions created a hostile relationship between Hagar and her mistress, Sarai. (Genesis 16:1-6).

After a harsh encounter with Sarai, Hagar fled toward Shur. In route, an angel of Yahweh appeared to Hagar at the well of a spring.

He instructed her to return to Sarai for she would bear a son who *"shall be a wild donkey of a man, his hand against everyone and everyone's hand against him, and he shall dwell over against all his kinsmen."* She was told to call her son Ishmael. Hagar then referred to God as "El-Roi," meaning that she had gone on seeing after God saw her. From that day, the well was called Beer-lahai-roi. She then did as she was instructed by returning to Abram in order to have her child. Abram was eighty-six years of age when Ishmael was born (Genesis 16:7-16).

Until this point, Sarah's name was actually Sarai. When Abraham was 99 years old, God spoke to him and blessed him with children and land. He changed his name from Abram to Abraham and his wife's name from Sarai to Sarah. God also promised Abraham that Sarah would have a child, and that God would maintain his covenant with this child, Isaac.

Three days later, three men approached Abraham's tent. He invited them in and Sarah went to prepare food for them. She was listening from the opening of the tent, when one of them (men who were really messengers from God) predicted that she would have a child. She laughed; after all, she was 90 years old and Abraham nearly 100! Yet, God predicted that in one year, she would give birth.

One year later, when Abraham was 100, Sarah's son, Isaac, was born. Once Isaac and Ishmael began to grow up, Sarah asked Abraham to send Hagar and Ishmael away and not to allow Ishmael to share an inheritance with Isaac. Biblical commentators disagree as to the reason why she did not want Ishmael in her house.

Some say Ishmael was worshipping other gods, others say he was teasing Isaac or bragging that, as firstborn, he would receive a double portion of the inheritance. God told Abraham to listen to Sarah and the next morning, Abraham sent Hagar and Ishmael away. Abraham rose early in the morning, gave Hagar some bread and water and sent her away with the boy. Hagar and Ishmael wandered in the wilderness of Beersheba. After they had finished drinking all the water in the bottle, Hagar, not wanting to see her son die of thirst, placed him under a shrub. Then she moved some distance away, crying and lamenting.

God heard her cries and sent an angel who told her not to fear and added that her son would grow up to be the ancestor of a great nation. God opened her eyes, and she saw a well nearby.

She filled her water bottle and gave the boy a drink.

Ishmael grew up in the wilderness, became a skilled archer, and married an Egyptian girl whom Hagar chose for him. Ishmael had 12 sons: Nebaioth, Kedar, Adbell, Mibsam, Mishma, Dumah, Massa, Hadad, Tema, Jetur, Napish, and Kedmah, all of them ancestors of great nations. His daughter, Mahalath—also called Basemath—married Esau son of Isaac. Ishmael died when he was 137 years old.

Thus God spared Ishmael as a result of His general promise, but the blessings pronounced on Ishmael are certainly inferior to the covenant blessings pronounced on Isaac (compare Genesis 17:21; 21; 12-13). We see that Ishmael was blessed, because he was the son of Abraham, but he was not the one through whom God's covenant blessings would be passed down. God kept His promise to make of Ishmael a great nation (21:18), but that is the limit.

Sarah lived to the age of 127 years (the only female in written Bible history in which her age at death is recorded) and died at

Hebron, southwest of Jerusalem. Abraham bought a burial cave (see Macpelah) from the Hittites, and Sarah was interred there (Genesis 23:1-20).

Eventually, Sarah's tomb was expanded and used as a family burial place, including not only Abraham but also for their son Isaac and his wife Rebekah, and then later their grandson Jacob (Israel) and his wife Leah (Genesis 49:29-32). They all remain there to this day awaiting their Resurrection.

Chapter Three

The Promised Son Isaac

God made other promises recorded in the Bible. Often He gave them in the form of covenants. A covenant is an agreement, compact or contract between two or more parties. In the Bible; however, the term implies more of a formal treaty like commitment to a relationship. In the covenants, God initiates; no negotiation of terms is allowed. God defines all of the conditions. The people could only accept or decline God's offer. They had no say in determining the framework of the covenant.

It should be obvious why God's covenants could not be negotiated agreements between equal parties. God is the Creator, and we are His creation. Our well-being is dependent on His love and favor. The New Oxford Dictionary of English defines the theological use of covenant as "an agreement which brings about a relationship with God and his people."

One of the most important covenants God made was with the Israelites, Abraham's descendants through his son Isaac and grandson Jacob (renamed Israel). The apostle Paul says of them: *"they are Israelites; theirs the adoption, the glory, the covenants, the giving of the law, the worship, and the promises;*

theirs the patriarchs, and from them, according to the flesh, is the Messiah." (Romans 9:4-5, New American Bible) (United Church of God Publication)

God's promise to Abraham was "dual"…a material promise and a spiritual one. The short version is: God promised Abraham "LAND" (specifically the WHOLE WORLD), the ultimate fulfillment of which shall be the "Kingdom of God" on the earth. *"There shall be weeping and gnashing of teeth, when ye SHALL SEE ABRAHAM, Isaac, and Jacob, and all the prophets, IN THE KINGDOM OF GOD, and you yourselves thrust out."* (Luke 13:28)

"For the PROMISE, that he shall be HEIR OF THE WORLD, was not to Abraham, or to his seed, through the law, but through the righteousness of faith." (Romans 4:13)

"Know ye therefore that they which are of faith, the same ARE THE CHILDREN OF ABRAHAM." (Galatians.3:7)

The spiritual PROMISE, of course, was and is: the CHRIST… and the SALVATION of the world!

"…I will BLESS them that BLESS thee… and in thee shall ALL THE FAMILIES OF THE EARTH BE BLESSED." (Genesis 12:3) That's the salvation of the nations.

It is Jesus who is bringing the Kingdom with Him when HE returns to the earth… and He's bringing His salvation with Him:

"…unto them that look for Him shall He appear the SECOND TIME without sin unto SALVATION." (Hebrews 9:28)

God's Promises to Abraham… (The Kingdom of God through His Seed, which is Christ)…is the same inheritance of Christians because:

"…IF YE BE CHRIST'S, then ye Abraham's seed, and HEIRS ACCORDING TO THE PROMISE." (Galatians 3:29)

And in the Judgment…all of the families of the generations of men will have to go through this same Christ to obtain this same inheritance…in order to enter into the Kingdom.

God's Promises

Hundreds of Bible prophecies tell us about the mission, purpose and ministry of Jesus Christ. The Scriptures are filled with prophecies of both His first and second coming.

"No longer shall your name be called Abram, but your name shall be Abraham; for I have made you a father of many nations." (Genesis 17:5; compare Romans 4:17-18)

What an astounding statement! God had a close relationship with Abraham and promised him that his descendants would ultimately comprise the nations. God even changed his name from Abram to Abraham, meaning "father of a multitude," to reflect the importance of this promise.

God made many promises to Abraham. The patriarch had such a close relationship with God that a Bible writer called him the *"Friend of God"* (James 2:23). Abraham's descendants also received several great and far reaching promises.

"And I will make your descendants as the dust of the earth; so that if a man could number the dust of the earth, then your descendants also could be numbered." (Genesis 15:5; 22:17)

Abraham's descendants were to number into multiple millions of people. Again, we see that God made some wonderful promises to this faithful servant.

The Covenant

Genesis 12:3-4

God made a covenant (contract) with Abraham. This covenant

was an unconditional one. God did not say, "Abraham, if you do certain things, then I will do certain things." God's promise to Abraham was unconditional. God said, *"Abraham, I WILL make of thee a great nation, and I WILL bless thee, and make thy name great; and thou SHALT be a blessing: and I WILL bless them that bless thee, and curse them that curse thee: and in thee shall all families of the earth be blessed."* (Genesis 12:2-3) There is no condition in the covenant for Abraham to fulfill. That is why it is an unconditional covenant. God promised to do these things and nothing could prevent it. The Covenant was fourfold:

(1) God would make Abraham's descendants a great nation.

(2) God would bless Abraham materially and make his name great.

(3) God would protect Abraham by blessing those that blessed him and cursing those who opposed Abraham.

(4) God would bless all the families of the earth through Abraham. God fulfilled His promise to Abraham.

The Blessings of a Great Nation

(1) Abraham's descendants became the nation of Israel. Until this very day the children of Abraham, the Jews, have remained an ethnically pure people. They are the only people on earth who can make that claim. It seems it would be impossible for a people to remain ethnically pure for 4,000 years. And in truth it would be, except that God made an unconditional promise to Abraham.

The continuing fulfillment of that covenant can be seen today. The Jews have been scattered all over the earth in every continent. Almost every city in the western world has a population of Jews. For example, many peoples from all over the world have come and settled in the United States. However, most immigrants in a generation or two lose their ethnic identity and become simply

"Americans." However, the Jews have remained a pure people and have retained their identity as Jews. Clearly, God has done this and is keeping His promise made to Abraham.

All the Material Blessings

(2) Abraham was richly blessed materially, and this promise was extended to his descendants as well. Although the Jewish people have suffered great persecutions throughout their history, they are not known as a poor people. Their power in Europe was the cause of Hitler's great hatred of them. At the heart of his plan for a new Germany and Europe was the elimination of all Jews and their influence in Europe.

Today, in the United States and Europe, the Jewish people are very powerful. They have great economic and political power. Although present day Israel is one of the smallest countries on the earth, it is one of the most powerful. Its economic, political and technological power rivals even that of the USA and Soviet Union. Surely, the hand of God is in all of this.

The name of Abraham is a world-renowned name. He is the father of not only the Jews, but of Christianity, and the entire Arab world as well. The three great religions of the world - Judaism, Christianity and Islam - all look to Abraham as their father. Apart from Jesus Christ, no name is as well- known as that of Abraham.

The Blessing of Protection

(3) God promised to bless those that blessed Israel and to curse those that cursed them. Every government that has persecuted the Jews has fallen even in modern times. The Russian government, which has had a national policy of persecution of the Jews, is in shambles. However, the United States, who has

always been a friend of the nation of Israel, has prospered greatly. No matter how intense the persecution of Israel God has protected them. In 1967, what is called the Six Day War, the tiny nation of Israel utterly destroyed all the combined efforts of the Arab nations which surrounded them. It has been called one of the greatest military victories in history. Against impossible odds they repelled everything the Arabs sent against them. They not only defeated these forces, but took great amounts of land including land in the south from the Gaza Strip to the Nile River, the West Bank and all of Jerusalem. Surely God's hand of protection is upon this small nation.

The Major Blessing to All the Families

(4) God also promised that all the families of the earth would be blessed through Abraham. History shows that the coming of the Messiah, the Lord Jesus Christ, changed the whole world. The history of western civilization is the history of the spread of Christianity. Even our calendar dates from the birth of Christ, the moral teachings of Christ and the New Testament, have shaped the western culture. The United States Constitution was based on Biblical standards and morals. Those nations which are identified as "Christian" have prospered greatly.

The greatest value of God's promise has been that, through the Lord Jesus, salvation is freely offered to the Gentiles (non-Jews). Today in this Church Age, God is saving mostly Gentiles. The Gospel is being carried around the world; however, not by the Jews, God's chosen people, but by the Gentiles. Among every nation on earth, men have heard the Good News (the meaning of the word "Gospel") and have received by faith, salvation through Jesus Christ.

We can see that God has kept His promise. Satan has done all he can to defect the plan of God, yet his efforts have been to no avail. God's promise stands and will stand until God's plan is completed.

It Began with ISAAC, the Chosen

Genesis 13:14-16

14) "And the LORD said unto Abram, after that Lot was separated from him, Lift up now your eyes, and look from the place where you are northward, and southward, and eastward, and westward:

15) "For all the land, which you see, to you will I give it, and to your seed forever.

16) "And I will make your seed as the dust of the earth: so that if a man can number the dust of the earth, then shall your seed also be numbered."

Genesis 15:1-8, 18

1) "After these things the Word of the LORD came to Abram in a vision, saying, 'Do not be afraid, Abram. I am your shield, your exceedingly great reward.'

2) "But Abram said, Lord GOD, what will You give me, seeing I go childless, and the heir of my house is Eliezer of Damascus?"

3) "Then Abram said, 'Look, You have given me no offspring; indeed one born in my house is my heir!'

4) "And behold, the Word of the LORD came to him, saying, 'This one shall not be your heir, but one who will come from your own body shall be your heir.'

5) "Then He brought him outside and said, 'Look now toward heaven, and count the stars if you are able to number them.' And He said to him, 'So shall your descendants be.'

6) "And he believed in the LORD, and He accounted it to him for righteousness.

36

18) *"In the same day the LORD made a covenant with Abram saying, unto your seed have I given this land, from the river of Egypt unto the great river, the river Euphrates:"*

Genesis 17:1:

When Abram was 99 years old, the LORD appeared to Abram and said to him, 'I am Almighty God; walk before Me and be blameless.'

2) "'And I will make My covenant between Me and you, and will multiply you exceedingly.'

3) "Then Abram fell on his face, and God talked with him, saying:

4) *'As for Me, behold, My covenant is with you, and you shall be a father of many nations.*

5) *"'No longer shall your name be called Abram, but your name shall be Abraham; for I have made you a father of many nations.*

6) *"'I will make you exceedingly fruitful; and I will make nations of you, and kings shall come from you.*

7) *"'And I will establish My covenant between Me and you and your descendants after you in their generations, for an everlasting covenant, to be God to you and your descendants after you.*

8) *"'Also I give to you and your descendants after you the land in which you are a stranger, all the land of Canaan, as an everlasting possession; and I will be their God.*

9) *And God said to Abraham: "As for you, you shall keep My covenant, you and your descendants after you throughout their generations.*

15) *Then God said to Abraham, 'As for Sarai your wife, you*

shall not call her name Sarai, but Sarah shall be her name.

16) "'And I will bless her and also give you a son by her; then I will bless her, and she shall be a mother of nations; kings of peoples shall be from her."

17) Then Abraham fell on his face and laughed, and said in his heart, 'Shall a child be born to a man who is one hundred years old? And shall Sarah, who is ninety years old, bear a child?

18) And Abraham said to God, 'Oh, that Ishmael might live before You!'"

19) Then God said: 'No, Sarah your wife shall bear you a son, and you shall call his name Isaac; I will establish My covenant with him for an everlasting covenant, and with his descendants after him.

20) "'And as for Ishmael, I have heard you. Behold, I have blessed him, and will make him fruitful, and will multiply him exceedingly. He shall beget twelve princes, and I will make him a great nation.'"

21) "'But My covenant I will establish with Isaac, whom Sarah shall bear to you at this set time next year.'"

Genesis 22:17-18

17) "'Blessing I will bless you, and multiplying I will multiply your descendants as the stars of the heaven and as the sand which is on the seashore; and your descendants shall possess the gate of their enemies.

18) "'In your seed all the nations of the earth shall be blessed, because you have obeyed My voice.'" Before Abraham even had any children, God told Abraham that He would give him a son by his wife, Sarah (Genesis 17:15-16). This son would be Isaac.

However, since she was barren, Sarah wrongly "took matters into her own hands" and gave her handmaiden slave, Hagar, to Abraham to bear him a son. Essentially, Abraham took a supernatural promise and "downgraded" it into a natural promise which is never a good idea when God is involved because it demonstrates a lack of faith.

Subsequently, God chose to give the inheritance, which He had promised Abraham (Abram) to Isaac, Abraham's second-born, rather than to Ishmael, his first-born (Genesis 17:18-21). This is because Isaac was the son God had promised to Abraham. Also, Ishmael was the son of Hagar, a slave woman; but Isaac was the son of Sarah, a free woman (Galatians 4:22-29).

Interestingly, after Abraham, demonstrating great humility and sacrifice, had been willing to give his son Isaac back to God, the Lord told Abraham that He would bless him greatly because he had not withheld his "only son" from God (Genesis 22:15-17). God called Isaac Abraham's only son, even though Abraham had an elder son, Ishmael. This was because Isaac was recognized by God as Abraham's only legitimate son – the son of the original promise.

Abraham had tried to get around being childless by taking matters into his own hands and producing children through the servant Hagar, and others, but Isaac is God's chosen. Isaac is the promised child of God born when Abraham is 100 years old and fully incapable of conceiving by natural means.

Isaac is a gift of grace, and his birth to extremely aged parents signifies the supernatural element in the birth of the covenant people. Against all odds God is shown to be absolutely faithful to his promises.

Chapter Four

Who Were Keturah & Her Sons

"Her name meant incense, invoking a sense of warmth and fragrance."

In our church we have begun to celebrate some of the main Jewish holidays. God has been revealing the importance of honoring His High and Holy Days. Because of the significance of the revelation around these days, we have chosen to honor and receive the special blessings as we obey the Lord.

Several years ago, we began celebrating the Passover, Pentecost in a new way, Rosh Shoshanna, the 10 Days of Awe, and learning more about the feast and Hanukkah. We are walking in the blessings of God as never before. We didn't know where it was going to take us, but we knew it was God and we needed to begin somewhere. We have begun to experience the pleasure of His presence in our lives as never before.

Through research, studies, and information given to us by several Jewish rabbis, we have found that the African people have Jewish roots that can be traced back to Abraham the patriarch of the Israelites.

Genesis 25:1-6:

1) "Abraham again took a wife, and her name was Keturah.

2) "And she bore him Zimran, Jokshan, Medan, Midian, Ishbak, and Shuah

3) "Jokshan begot Sheba and Dedan. And the sons of Dedan were Asshurim, Letushim, and Leummim.

4) "And the sons of Midian were Ephah, Epher, Hanoch, Abidah, and Eldah. All these were the children of Keturah.

5) "And Abraham gave all that he had to Isaac.

6) "But Abraham gave gifts to the sons of the concubines which Abraham had; and while he was still living he sent them eastward, away from Isaac his son, to the country of the east."

(1 Chronicles 1:32) The sons of Keturah, Abraham's concubine; she bore Zimran, and Jokshan, and Medan, and Midian, and Ishbak, and Shuah. The sons of Jokshan: Sheba, and Dedan. (WEB KJV JPS ASV BBE DBY WBS YLT NAS NIV)

(1 Chronicles 1:33) The sons of Midian: and Epher, and Hanoch, and Abida, and Eldaah. All these were sons of Keturah. (WEB KJV JPS ASV BBE DBY WBS YLT NAS NIV)

According to the Hebrew Bible, Keturah, or Ketura, was the woman whom Abraham, the patriarch of the Israelites, married after the death of his wife Sarah. Her nationality is Ethiopian as she was the mother of Sheba and the Medians whose descendant Jethro, or Ragu'el or Reu'el, the Ethiopian Priest of Median, begot a daughter Zipporah, who in the Scriptures, was referred to as the Ethiopian wife of Moses.

History has largely forgotten Keturah. She was Abraham's second wife, if Hagar isn't counted. Unlike Sarah, she had six sons. She does not appear to have had much role in the lineage of Christ. The Bible doesn't say exactly when Keturah became Abraham's wife. If it was after Sarah's death, Abraham would have been quite elderly.

Keturah is one of the most evocative names in the Bible. It means perfumed or incense, and brings to mind the burning aroma of the sacrifices and the incense smoke that ascended as a sweet offering to the Lord.

Keturah bore Abraham six sons, Zimran, Jokshan, Medan, Midian, Ishbak, and Shuah. Keturah was the other of six sons, representing Arabian tribes south and east of Canaan, so that through the offspring of Keturah, Abraham became "the father of many nations" including the Ethiopians.

We have here an account of his children by Keturah, another wife, which he married after the death of Sarah. He had buried Sarah, and married Isaac, the two dear companions of his life, and was now solitary. His family wanted a governess and it was not good for him to be alone. He, therefore, marries Keturah, probably the chief of his maid servants born in his house or bought with money.

His six sons with her built on the promise made to Abraham concerning the great increase of his posterity. The strength he received by the promise still remained in him, to show how much the virtue of the promise exceeds the power of nature.

To the sons of Hagar and Keturah, Abraham gave gifts; probably cattle for breed, seed to sow the land and implement for husbandry.

And sent he them away while he was still alive. It is believed that he did this before his death so that after his death they would dispute a settlement in the Land of Promise with Isaac. Abraham very prudently sent them to procure settlements during his lifetime, that they might be under no temptation to dispute the settlement with Isaac in Canaan.

From this situation arose the law which has prevailed in almost all countries of giving the estates to the eldest son by a lawful wife.

It was perfectly legitimate in those ancient times, yet their children did not inherit, except in case of failure of legal issues, and with the consent of the lawful wife. By law, all natural children were excluded from the paternal inheritance but their fathers were permitted to give them any sum not beyond a thousand drachma by way of a present, eastward, unto the east country - Arabia Deserta, which was eastward of Beer-sheba, where Abraham lived.

Was Keturah Abraham's Wife or Concubine?

Although Keturah is mentioned only four times in the Bible (in two different sections of Scripture - Genesis 25:1, 4; 1 Chronicles 1:32-33), her relationship to Abraham has come under severe scrutiny.

Skeptics have charged the Bible writers with erring in regard to their portrayal of Keturah. Allegedly, Genesis 25:1 and 1 Chronicles 1:32 are contradictory because the first passage indicates Keturah as Abraham's "wife," while the other says she was Abraham's "concubine." Based upon the understanding of some that there is a distinction of the words "wife" (Hebrew 'issa) and "concubine" (pileges) during the monarchic period, even some Bible believers may be somewhat perplexed at the different titles given to Keturah.

Was she Abraham's wife, or was she his concubine?

Many are aware that during David's reign as Israel's king, he had "wives" and "concubines" (2 Samuel 19:5). Also, during Solomon's kingship, "he had seven hundred wives, princesses, and three hundred concubines" (pileges) are distinct terms that rarely, if ever, are used interchangeably. Such begs the question, "Why Keturah was called Abraham's wife in one passage, and his concubine in another?" Are these two sections of Scripture really contradictory as Bible critics would have believed?

First, for Genesis 25:1 and 1 Chronicles 1:32-33 to be a contradiction, one must know whether or not these passages are referring to the same time. It is possible that Keturah was Abraham's "concubine" in the beginning, and then became his "wife" at a later time. If such were the case, Bible writers could legitimately use both terms when describing her.

Second, although it was unusual for the terms "wives" and "concubine" to be used interchangeably during the monarchic period, evidence indicates that in patriarchal times, using these terms to refer to the same person was somewhat normal. Consider the following: And Abraham gave all that he had to Isaac.

But Abraham gave gifts to the sons of the concubines, which Abraham had, and while he was still living he sent them eastward, away from Isaac his son, to the country of the east. (Genesis 25:5-6)

Isaac, son of Sarah, was set apart from all of Abraham's other sons, which were born to him by his concubines. By implication,

Keturah, who was not the mother of Isaac, was described as a concubine. (1 Chronicles 1:32)

Bilhah, Rachel's maid (Genesis 29:29), was one of Jacob's "concubines" (35:22). But, she also was called his "wife" both before and after she gave birth to two of Jacob's sons. (Genesis 30:4; 37:2)

Genesis 16:3 calls Hagar Abraham's "wife" ('issa), while Genesis 25:6 implies that Hagar, Sarah's maidservant, also was his "concubine).

Although Genesis 25:1 says, "Abraham again took a wife" (Keturah), verse 6 of that same chapter indicates Keturah also was his concubine.

Hebrew scholar Victor Hamilton believes this concubine-wife relationship to be dissimilar to what was seen during the days of David and Solomon. It is reasonable to conclude that this "co-identification" in Genesis indicates "that the concubines of Abraham and Jacob were not pilagsim [concubines-EL] in the later sense, but that no term was available for that type of concubinage; thus pileges and issa were used as synonyms to describe these women the patriarchal narratives." [What reference does this come from?](1990, p. 446)

In an article that the late Semitist, Dr. Chaim Rabin, wrote regarding the origin pileges, he stated: "By alternating the terms within the easily apprehended framework of a story, a similar impression of "in-betweenness was created." [reference?](1974, p. 364)

Keturah was a concubine-wife. It seems that that she was more than a concubine (often considered a second-rate wife of servant status), but not on a par with Sarah, Abraham's first "wife" and mother of the promised son (Genesis 17:15-22). Just as Bilhah, Jacob's concubine-wife, did not rival Rachel or Leah,

Keturah was not equivalent with Sarah.

Thus, Bible writers were not mistaken when referring to Keturah and Bilbah as both wives and concubines; they simply used two words to indicate the "in-between" position of the women.

Although I agree with most of the information above, I believe that Keturah was Abraham's wife. She was not the wife to carry the promised child. Nevertheless, she had children from Abraham and these children were also the seed of Abraham. These sons were also a part of God's promise.

(Genesis 17:4) *"As for Me, behold, My covenant is with you, and you shall be a father of many nations."*

(Genesis 17:5) *"No longer shall your name be called Abram, but your name shall be Abraham; for I have made you a father of many nations."*

(Romans 4:17-18) "as it is written, *"I have made you a father of many nations"*) in the presence of Him whom he believed— God, who gives life to the dead and calls those things which do not exist as though they did;

18) *who, contrary to hope, in hope believed, so that he became the father of many nations, according to what was spoken, "So shall your descendants be."*

Genesis 25:1 discusses who some of those other nations are that Abraham would father.

Genesis 25:1-6

1) "Abraham again took a wife, and her name was Keturah

2) And she bore Zimran, Jokshan, Medan, Midian, Ishbak, and Shuah.

3) "Jokshan begot Sheba and Dedan. And the sons of Dedan were Asshurim, Letushim, and Leummim.

4) "And the sons of Midian were Ephah Epher, Hanoch,

Abidah, and Eldaah. All these were the children of Keturah.

5) "And Abraham gave all that he had to Isaac.

6) "But Abraham gave gifts to the sons of the concubines which Abraham had; and while he was still living he sent them eastward, away from Isaac his son, to the country of the east." It is said that Keturah's sons were mighty men in their own right and were as strong as oxen. Several Jewish rabbis believe that Abraham sent Keturah's sons away in fear of them over taking Isaac, the promised one.

The Sons of Keturah and Abraham

Zimran

Personal name meaning "vine dresser" celebrated in song "famous" or "mountain goat." Son of Abraham and Keturah and ancestor of an Arabian tribe (Genesis 25:2: 2; 1 Chronicles 1:32), possibly identified with Zabram, located somewhere west of Mecca on the Red Sea, and with Zimri (Jeremiah 25:25). So Zimran **was a musician, a singer, a songwriter, and he was famous for his music.** "One Who Makes Music," gardens, or keeps mountain sheep. He was a shepherd who tended and guarded his flock.

Jokshan

Jokshan is a son of Abraham with Keturah. The name Medan comes from (yaqosh 906) originally meaning to set a trap or snare. This verb occurs 40 times, most often metaphorically, meaning ensnaring people (1 Samuel 18:21, Psalm 18:5, Jeremiah 5:26). He was a trapper of animals. The name Jokshan means "One Who Sets A Snare, or Fowler." *Jones' Dictionary of Old Testament Proper Names* also derives this name from the above mentioned verb, and renders the name Jokshan as "sportsman," possibly assuming that Jokshan was hunting for fun. **Jokshan was into sports. He was an athlete.**

Medan

Medan is a son of Abraham with Keturah. The name Medan comes from the verb (din 426c) meaning **strife and contention**. The name Medan differs only slightly from the name of his brother Midian. Four centuries later Moses flees from Egypt to the land of Midian. There he meets Jethro, the priest of Midian, and marries his daughter Zipporah. Medan and Midian had to do with the law; they were thought to be contentious because they wanted to plead or judge on one's behalf.

Ishbak

Ishbak is a son of Abraham with Keturah (Genesis 25:2). According to *BDB Theological Dictionary, NOBS Study Bible Name List and Fuerst's Hebrew & Chaldee* lexicon to the Old Testament, the name Ishbak comes from the Aramaic (shabaq 3018) meaning to tear asunder, reduce to fragments, loosen, unbind, or set free. When Jesus, on the cross, cries His famous 'Eli, Eli, lama sabachtani?' (Matthew 27:46), He quotes Psalm 22:1 but in Aramaic. The original Hebrew uses the verb (azab 1594), which means to leave, forsake, loose. This verb is used in all kind of ways, mostly as to be expected. The name Ishbak means abandoned or set free. *NOBS Study Bible Name List* reads "leaving." *Jones' Dictionary of Old Testament Proper Names* regards this name as a future form of the verb and curiously renders **he was a deliverer**.

Shuah

There are four different Hebrew names that transliterated into English form the name Shuah, or variations of it depending on the translation. Shoa (or variations of) is spelled the same as one of the Shuah's, but pronounced slightly different. The first Shuah (pronounced shuach) is a son of Abraham with Keturah (Genesis 25:2), and the name Shoa occurs in Ezekiel 23:23 where it is the name of a Chaldean tribe.

The names come from the verb (shuah 2343.1), meaning be bowed down or humble (according to *HAW Theological Wordbook of the Old Testament*) and sink down (according to *BDB Theological Dictionary*). The name of this son of Abraham (Genesis 25:2) and the name of this perhaps female descendant of Judah (1 Chronicles 4:11) mean "brought low" or "put in a pit."

The name looks exactly like the verb (shawa 2348) cry out (for help). Derivatives are (shua' 2348a), a cry (for help); (shoa" 2348b), a cry (for help); (shaw' a 2348c), a cry (for help). *BDB Theological Dictionary* lists the SHOA as mentioned in Ezekiel and reads rich for Shoa and prosperity for all variations of Shuah. **Shua was the one who cried out to the Lord for help. He was an intercessor and his prayers would be answered which caused them to be prosperous.**

Jokshan's children: Sheba

There are two completely different names in the Bible that both transliterate into English as Sheba. The first Sheba, with aleph mentioned in the Bible, is a son of Raamah, son of Cush, son of Ham, and son of Noah. Another Sheba is a son of Joktan, who is the brother of Peleg (Genesis 10:28). Thirdly, there is a son of Jokshan, son of Abraham with Keturah. Sheba is also a region or nation of which the queen journeyed to Solomon (1 Kings 10:1; Matthew 12:42). This is the name Sheba according to *Jones' Dictionary of Old Testament Proper.*

BDB Theological Dictionary sees relations with a verb that means "to make campaign or expedition." The name may even mean (shaba 2311) "to take captive." **His name means one who wages war or is an explorer and then takes one captive.**

Dedan

The name Dedan comes possibly from the Hebrew noun (ddd405), meaning breast or nipple, or the Hebrew verb (dada 406), meaning to move slowly or lead slowly (Psalm 42:5, Isaiah 38:15). It may even have to do with (dwd 410) the root for beloved (aunt, uncle, even the name David).

Jones' Dictionary of Old Testament Proper Names goes with (dada 406) and reads leading forward, i.e. great increase of family. *The NOBS Study Bible Name List* reads low, for no discernible reason. *BDB Theological Dictionary* does not translate. **Dedan was a leader and is one that leads slowly and knows how to grow and have great increase.**

Dedans' sons: Asshurim The name Asshurim is a plural of the name Asshur.

Asshur is a son of Shem, son of Noah (Genesis 10:22). This Asshur is also the progenitor of the Assyrians, which are sometimes referred to as simply Asshur (see Numbers 24:22 or Ezekiel 27:23). Another group (of much later, Abrahamic origin) named after the name Asshur is the Asshurim (Genesis 25:3). Another Asshur is mentioned in 1 Chronicles 2:24, in the genealogy of Judah.

The name Asshur is highly similar to the Hebrew name Asher but is spelled with waw before the resh [not sure this is understandable?]. However, *BDB Theological Dictionary* reports a connection with the Hebrew verb (yashar 930), be level, straight up, or just. *NOBS Study Bible Name List* seems to agree and reads level plain. *Jones' Dictionary of Old Testament Proper Names* derives the name Asshur from the verb (ashr 183) meaning "to go straight on" and which also yields the name Asher. *Jones'* renders the name Asshur, "a step." **Therefore, Asshur was one that was just, righteous, and level headed.**

Letushim

The name Letushim is the plural form of the verb (latish 1110), hammer, sharpen forge, or push. This verb is not very widely used, so it probably means something specific for a hard-working society. What that is we do not really know, but the various contexts suggest there is no single English equivalent of this verb.

In Genesis 4:22 we read about Tubal Cain who is a hammerer of bronze and iron. In 1 Samuel 13:20, the Israelites go down to the Philistines, each to sharpen his plowshare, his mattock and his hoe. The usage occurs in Psalm 7:12, where God sharpens His sword and bends his bow against a man who does not repent. In Psalm 52:2, a mighty man's destructive tongue is compared to a sharpened razor. Job even complains that his enemy has sharpened his eyes at him (16:9). The name Letushim means **"sharp or sharpened."**

Leummim

The name Leummim is the plural form of the unused root. Although this root is not used in the Bible, it is a familiar Semitic root (the Arabic word la'ama means assemble). Derivatives of this root used in the Bible and mean nations, or people (leom 1069a). Other words for people are: (goy 326e), which denotes corporeality (used in the name Haroseth-hagovin), and (am 1640a), which refers to a group of people that are related (as used in the names Amram, Amalek, Rehoboam, and possibly Gomorrah).

The name Leummim means "nations of peoples."

Midian's sons: Ephah

The name Ephah occurs three times in the Bible. The first Ephah is a son of Midian, son of Abraham with Keturah (Genesis 2:46). The second Ephah is a concubine of Caleb (1 Chronicles 2:46). The third Ephah is mentioned in the genealogy of Judah (1Chronicles 2:47). The name Ephah comes from the Hebrew root group ('up 1582-1583):

*The verb ('up 1582), **meaning to fly.** This verb is used for birds (Isaiah 31:5) and angels (Isaiah 6:2). Derivative ('op 1582a) denotes flying creatures; insects (Leviticus 11:20) and birds (Genesis 78:27). Derivative ('ap'ap 1582b) means eyelid in all the straight-forward uses of the body part (Psalm 132:4), but also, curiously enough, as the **"eyelids of dawn," i.e. the breaking of dawn (Job 3:9).**

Epher

There are three Ephers mentioned in the Bible. The first Epher is a son of Midian, son of Abraham with Keturah (Genesis 25:4). Other Ephers are a descendant of Judah (1 Chronicles 4:17) and a family head of Manasseh (1 Chronicles 5:24). The name Epher is identical to the Hebrew root group (aphar 1664-1665).

• The verb (apar 1664) basically covers actions that can be done with dust: throw it perhaps, grind something (2

Samuel 16:13; build something (Genesis 26:15), even make potions from it (Numbers 5:17). The derivative ('apar 1664a) means dust, earth, ashes, etc. This is the same word as used to describe creation's basic fabric: dust of the earth (Genesis 2:7).

- The noun ('oper 1665a), meaning stag. *HAW Theological Wordbook of the Old Testament* adds as a note, "apar, 'dust, comes from a different root than the noun oper, 'young hart, stag,' and the name Epher."

The name Epher may come from the noun, meaning dust, and that's not unprecedented as the name Adam means "ade from Earth." In that sense, Epher means **dustling**.

All the consulted sources; however, go with the meaning of stag: *NOBS Study Bible name List* reads **young deer**. *Jones' Dictionary of Old Testament Proper Names* reads a young heart.

Hanoch

There are two Hanochs in the Bible. One is a son of Midian, son of Abraham with Keturah (Genesis 25:4). The other is a son of Reuben, son of Jacob (Genesis 46:9).

This name Hanoch is closely similar to that of Enoch. Both names come from (hanak 693) meaning dedicate, or begin. Since the names Enoch and Hanoch are so similar, *Jones' Dictionary of Old Testament Proper Names* doesn't even treat Hanoch as a separate name. *NOBS Study Bible Name List* reads dedicated for both Enoch and Hanoch. **Hanoch was dedicated to God**.

Abidah-Abida

Abida is a son of Midian who is a son of Abraham with Keturah (Genesis 25:4). The name Abida is a compilation of two elements:

1) Abi, from the Hebrew word (ab 4a), meaning basically father (hence abba, papa, pope), but with applications beyond the contemporary use of father. Many times 'ab is used as counselor or judge (Genesis 45:8, 2 Kings 2:12). Abi (with yod) appears frequently in connection with names of places to express the lord of a county, city or village.

2) And the Hebrew word (dea 848a) meaning knowledge, opinion. This noun is derived from the verb (yada 848) to know, expressing a multitude of shades of knowledge gained by the senses (*HAW Theological Wordbook of the Old Testament*). This reference can be found in Deuteronomy 34:10 andIsaiah 1:3; but most important in Proverbs 1:7.

The name **Abida means "father of knowledge"** (*Jones' Dictionary of Old Testament Proper Names*), the father knows (*NOBS Study Bible Name List*) or my father took knowledge (*BDB theological Dictionary*).

Eldaah

The name Eldaah occurs only once in the Bible, as a son of Midian, son of Abraham with Keturah (Genesis 25:4).

The name Eldaah is a compilation of two elements. The first part is the word (El 93), El, the common abbreviation of Elohim, the genus God. The origin of the second part of the name Eldaah is unclear. *Jones' Dictionary of Old Testament Proper Names and NOBS Study Bible Name List* lists it, but which is supposed to be similar to a certain Arabian verb that means to call; therefore, the **meaning "God has called."**

Fuerst's Hebrew & Chaldee lexicon to the Old Testament and Klein's Etymological dictionary of the Hebrew Language relate to the Hebrew noun (dea 848b), meaning knowledge, which comes from the verb from (yada 848) meaning to know. What the original name giver meant to say with the name Eldaah (and in which language) is no longer clear. But for a Hebrew audience, the name Eldaah would have meant Knowledge of God, or, slightly more daring: **God is Knowledge.**

4) And the sons of Midian were Ephah Epher, Hanoch, Abidah, and Eldaah. All these were the children of Keturah.

As we can see the sweet smelling aroma, Keturah brought forth some sons who had been created to do some major things for the Lord. These young men went on to become great kings, princes, priests, warriors, law-givers, shepherds and hunters, just to name a few of their conquests.

I understand that every culture has a place in the kingdom, and that place cannot be filled by any other culture or race in the Kingdom of God. I desire to see that all cultures fulfill their Godly assignments, receive their kingdom inheritance and take their place in the Kingdom of God. I want to do all within my power to see this desire fulfilled. I believe that in writing this book, the African and Hispanic cultures will get some clarity about their identity in the kingdom. Each culture needs the other. There is no fullness of the kingdom until we all come together with understanding while honoring one another.

Chapter 5

Spirit of Amalek

When I was in Oklahoma in April 2010 at the Heartland Apostolic Prayer Network Conference, Prophet Chuck Pierce and Apostle Barbara Wentroble prophesied over me as the multicultural affairs leader for the nation in that organization. They gave me many words about specific things God wanted me to do while in my position.

Prophet Chuck told me that the issues in America were not black and white issues (meaning races). But that the root of all racism was an anti-Semitic spirit. An anti-Semitic spirit is a spirit sent by Satan that hates the Jewish people with a perfect hate. This spirit has tried to persecute God's people, the Jews, in order to eliminate them so that the promised seed would not come forth and that the second coming of Jesus would be prevented. The goal of this spirit is total destruction of the Jews.

(Exodus 17:8) *Now Amalek came and fought with Israel (in Rephidim. 9) And Moses said to Joshua, "Choose us some men and go out, fight with Amalek. Tomorrow I will stand on the top of the hill with the rod of God in my hand."*

10) So Joshua did as Moses said to him, and fought with Amalek. And Moses, Aaron, and Hur went up to the top of the hill. 11) And so it was, when Moses held up his hand, that Israel prevailed; and when he let down his hand, Amalek prevailed. 12)

But Moses' hands [became] heavy; so they took a stone and put [it] under him, and he sat on it. And Aaron and Hur supported his hands, one on one side, and the other on the other side; and his hands were steady until the going down of the sun.

13) So Joshua defeated Amalek and his people with the edge of the sword. 14) Then the LORD said to Moses, "Write this [for] a memorial in the book and recount [it] in the hearing of Joshua that I will utterly blot out the remembrance of Amalek from under heaven." 15) And Moses built an altar and called its name, The-LORD-Is-My-Banner; 16) **for he said, "Because the LORD has sworn: the LORD [will have] war with Amalek from generation to generation."**

If we go to the book of Esther we have a good example of this anti-Semitic spirit in action.

(Esther 3:1-6) 1) After these things King Ahasuerus promoted Haman, the son of Hammedatha the Agagite, and advanced him and set his seat above all the princes who [were] with him. 2) And all the king's servants who [were] within the king's gate bowed and paid homage to Haman, for so the king had commanded concerning him. But Mordecai would not bow or pay homage. 3) Then the king's servants who [were] within the king's gate said to Mordecai, "Why do you transgress the king's command?" 4) Now it happened, when they spoke to him daily and he would not listen to them, that they told [it] to Haman, to see whether Mordecai's words would stand; for [Mordecai] had told them that he [was] a Jew. 5) When Haman saw that Mordecai did not bow or pay him homage, Haman was filled with wrath. 6) But he disdained to lay hands on Mordecai alone, for they had told him of the people of Mordecai. Instead, Haman sought to destroy all the Jews who [were] throughout the whole kingdom

of Ahasuerus--the people of Mordecai.

You may know the story of Esther and how she was strategically placed to save the children of Israel. You may remember how Haman was so insistent on destroying the Jews. The question becomes who was Haman and why did he really want to destroy the Jews? Well, Haman was a descendant of Agag who was the king of the Amalekites. There are many situations in Scripture that involves the Amalekites. In the book of Samuel, the Prophet Samuel told King Saul to kill the Amalekites for what they had done to Israel. What did they do? In I Samuel 15:1-3, it says *Samuel also said to Saul, "The LORD sent me to anoint you king over His people, over Israel. Now therefore, heed the voice of the words of the LORD. 2) "Thus says the LORD of hosts: 'I will punish Amalek [for] what he did to Israel, how he ambushed him on the way when he came up from Egypt. 3) 'Now go and attack Amalek, and utterly destroy all that they have, and do not spare them. But kill both man and woman, infant and nursing child, ox and sheep, camel and donkey.'"*

Then in verses 7-9 it says:

7) And Saul attacked the Amalekites, from Havilah all the way to Shur, which is east of Egypt.

8) He also took Agag king of the Amalekites alive, and utterly destroyed all the people with the edge of the sword.

9) But Saul and the people spared Agag and the best of the sheep, the oxen, the fatlings, the lambs, and all [that was] good, and were unwilling to utterly destroy them. But everything despised and worthless, that they utterly destroyed.

So here is where King Saul didn't obey the voice of the Lord our God. God said for him to utterly destroy the Amalekites and all that they have. King Saul killed the people and kept alive

King Agag and took some of the livestock.

Verses 19-23

19) *"Why then did you not obey the voice of the LORD? Why did you swoop down on the spoil, and do evil in the sight of the LORD?"*

20) *And Saul said to Samuel, "But I have obeyed the voice of the LORD, and gone on the mission on which the LORD sent me, and brought back Agag king of Amalek; I have utterly destroyed the Amalekites.*

21) *"But the people took of the plunder, sheep and oxen, the best of the things which should have been utterly destroyed, to sacrifice to the LORD your God in Gilgal."*

22) *So Samuel said: "Has the LORD [as great] delight in burnt offerings and sacrifices, as in obeying the voice of the LORD? Behold, to obey is better than sacrifice, [And] to heed than the fat of rams.*

23) *For rebellion [is as] the sin of witchcraft, and stubbornness [is as] iniquity and idolatry. Because you have rejected the word of the LORD, He also has rejected you from [being] king."*

As a result of King Saul's disobedience God rejected him from being king. As a prisoner in the Jewish tradition, a king was still treated with royal courtesies and was given a nice place to live. He was given the choices of concubines to reproduce with and much more. King Agag was living in the land of Israel which was bad enough in itself but he was also having unions with Israelite maidens and reproducing little Agag's.

How many of us know that partial obedience is still disobedience. The problems with Agag and the Amalekites started in the book of Exodus and were recorded in (Deuteronomy 25: 17-19)

17) "Remember what Amalek did to you on the way as you were coming out of Egypt, 18) "how he met you on the way and attacked your rear ranks, all the stragglers at your rear, when you [were] tired and weary; and he did not fear God.

19) "Therefore it shall be, when the LORD your God has given you rest from your enemies all around, in the land which the LORD your God is giving you to possess [as] an inheritance, [that] you will blot out the remembrance of Amalek from under heaven. You shall not forget.

Anti-semiticism (also spelled anti-semitism or anti-Semitism) is prejudice, hatred of, or discrimination against Jews for reasons connected to their Jewish heritage. A person who holds such positions is called an "anti-Semite," one who discriminates against, is hostile toward or prejudiced against Jews. This is the same spirit behind all prejudices; it hates women, it hates people of color and it hates the Jews. It is the spirit operating in the Muslims and any other anti-Christ organization. It hates Jesus because He is a Jew, which liberated women and other cultures.

The Amalekites where the first ones to attack Israel after they crossed the Red Sea. They were the bitterest enemy of Israel and they had genetic evil engrained in their ancestry bloodline.

But the Amalekites even go further back. The first mention of a person called Amalek in the Bible was in the genealogies of Esau, the brother of Jacob. Amalek was born and raised in a family that was full of immorality, incest, and hatred on both sides.

What did God say about Amalek? He did not fear God. What did God say about the descendants of Amalek? "That you will blot the remembrance of Amalek from under heaven."

Amalek had to be dealt with again and again. The spirit of Amalek is the frontal assault against the Almighty God and His chosen people literal and spiritual Israel. (Exodus 17:16) God has sworn by His throne, God is at war with Amalek for all generations.

This spirit hates the Jews and any of God's people. This spirit hates black people, it hates Hispanics, and it hates anyone that has anything to do with God.

This spirit works with irrational hatred, violence, rage, resentment, murder, and revenge. It works with pride, greed, defiance, disobedience, seduction, jealousy and deception and much more. It likes to torture people. It is satanically inspired.

It is the spirit behind Islam. It was the spirit behind the holocaust. It is the spirit behind slavery in the U.S. It was the same spirit that tried to annihilate the Native Americans. It is the spirit behind terrorism. It is the same spirit that hates women, and it is the same spirit in the church today that refuses to line up with Israel.

It is an attitude of hate and hatred today against certain people or groups. It is not your white brother or sister that you should be fighting. It is not your African-American brother and sister that you should be fighting. It is not your Hispanic brother or sister that you should be fighting. It is not your Asian neighbor that you should be against. It is not the Hindu person at your school you should be fighting. It is not even the Muslins we should be fighting.

Prophet Chuck told us to look again.... "Church we need to look again and see who the real fight is with. Look again! Look again! Look Again!"

It is the spirit of Amalek. It is the spirit of Amalek!

The children of Israel had to deal with Amalek.

God is also asking us to look again into our own hearts. I know most of us are real high and holy and don't need any deliverance but God asked me to look again and make sure I don't have any trace of Amalek in my own heart. He wants us to look again to ensure that we are not deceived about prejudices and racism.

Moses and Joshua had to deal with Amalek and when they did, as long as Moses' arms were in the arms of Joshua, they would win. But when his arms came down Joshua would lose. This was an illustration of intercession. So church, as long as the **intercessors are praying,** we will defeat Amalek. If the intercessors stop praying, Amalek will defeat us.

So I say intercessors to this call of intercession, I say awake intercessors and pray against Amalek so we can win this war in our nation.

King David had to deal with Amalek. The Amalekites came and took David's wives, took his, children, took his money, took his cattle and took everything he had. But not only his stuff, but they took all of the warriors stuff, too. And David inquired of the Lord, and the Lord took David to go and pursue and take back everything. God said you shall recover all.

And somebody today needs to pursue Amalek because he has come up in your house and has taken your children, your wife, your husband, and your money. I hear the Lord say pursue and you shall recover all. But not only did David get his stuff back, but he got all the wealth from all the battles the Amalekites had fought. And it shall be so with you!

David and Barak had to deal with the Amalekites. **Esther and Mordecia** had to deal with the Amalek. **Psalm 83** talks about the Amalekites forming a confederacy against God's people.

And today you and I must deal with Amalekites. Of Amalek in Exodus 17:16 for he said, *"Because the LORD has sworn: the LORD [will have] war with Amalek from generation to generation."*

With that being said, it is high time we awake to the fact that God wants us to work together to advance His Kingdom and that this gospel is for every nation, every tribe, every tongue and all people. And everyone has a part to play.

It is high time we awake to the truth behind racism and deal with it, and no longer let the spirit of deception operate in our lives. It has short circuited our power and our success in advancing the Kingdom.

It is high time we awake to the fact:

(Ephesians 6:12) – *"For we wrestle not against flesh and blood, but against principalities, against powers, against the rulers of the darkness of this age, against spiritual [hosts] of wickedness in the heavenly [places]."*

It is high time that we awake to the fact: *"For the weapons of our warfare are not carnal but mighty in God for pulling down strongholds"*

It is high time that that we awake to the fact: that God says, I would not have you ignorant of the wiles or schemes of the devil.

Your enemy is not your neighbor.

It is high time that we awake to the fact: That we have power and authority over this enemy.

(Luke 10:19) - *"Behold, I give you the authority to trample on serpents and scorpions, and over all the power of the enemy, and nothing shall by any means hurt you."*

It is high time that that we awake and come together to defeat this enemy once and for all. Remember, one can chase a 1,000, and 10 can put 10,000 to flight.

It is high time that we awake and come into the true unity that God has wanted for us since the beginning of time.

(Psalm 133:1-3)

1) Behold, how good and how pleasant [it is], For brethren to dwell together in unity!

2) [It is] like the precious oil upon the head, Running down on the beard, the beard of Aaron, Running down on the edge of his garments.

3) [It is] like the dew of Hermon, Descending upon the mountains of Zion; for there the LORD commanded the blessing--Life forevermore.

Do you remember the people at the Tower of Babel how they came together to build a building to the sky…And looked down from heaven and said I better confuse their language because the people are one and there won't be anything that they will not be able to do?

It is high time that that we awake and understand that God wants us to put down prejudices and all racism against each other and begin to honor one another. Be kindly affectionate to one another with brotherly love, and in honor giving preference to one another.

Let's look again church, let's look again! Prejudices have become idols in our lives because anything we put before God is idolatry. Our mindsets, our perspectives if they are not God's perspectives they have become idolatry.

It is high time that that we awake and understand that we will never walk in the fullness of the power, and glory and, dominion of the kingdom until we stop Amalek and let every tribe, every tongue, and every nation take its rightful place in the kingdom.

It is high time that that we awake and make the decision in Georgia that the buck stops here, and we will no longer let Amalek prevail against us!!!!

When I went to my last deliverance session in Oklahoma City with Dr. Pat Legako several years ago, (I know some of you are so holy and good you only needed one deliverance session 25 years ago and no more. But I'm always getting delivered of stuff), I was there and Ressie said you have an inner war going on. She said your Caucasian blood, and your Native American blood and your African blood within you are at war. I had an inner war because of the different races within me. They bound the racism and some other stuff and my spirit came into a place of peace. I have been free from racism every since. I was a picture of the body of Christ. There is an inner war within the body but God is saying it is time for this inner war to end today in the United States which will eventually go out into the nations.

Prophet Chuck said that Atlanta would be the headquarters of a major revolution. But I saw God blow on the **root of revolution** starting in our nation up north. And I saw this area becoming the **headquarters of a major revolution** that would change the course of this nation. When it hit Atlanta it mingled with the seeds of the revolution of the Civil Rights Movement. I see Black America rising up and leading our nation and with that it is going to create a revolution. (Prophet Chuck Pierce 10-2-06)

We all got nervous about Black America leading this nation and none of us knew what this meant. But today I can tell you what it means. It means African-Americans will lead in forgiveness, they will lead in humility, they will lead in love, they will lead in peace, and they will lead in joy.

This will continue to defeat Amalek because we will come in an opposite spirit of hatred, violence, anger, pride, and confusion. It doesn't mean we will not wage war against him. But we will continue to overcome by love.

We are going to break the power of this thing from over our nation today.

We pray Father in the name of Jesus, Yeshuah; we come in humility asking forgiveness for allowing this spirit of Amalek to operate in our lives in anyway. Lord help us look again and seek if there are areas in our lives that we have overlooked where this spirit may be operating in us.

But now we come with Apostolic Authority and we bind the spirit of Amalek, we break the power of the spirit of Amalek from over the state and nation, and we cast him out of the states and command him to go to the place that Jesus has appointed him to go to.

Jesus went to hell and got the keys of death, and He said greater works shall you do because I go to the Father. So we go in the spirit realm to the core of the earth under our state to the gates of hell and we shut the gate that has been allowing this spirit and his imps to come from underground and operate in the land and in the people of our state.

And likewise we take authority of the atmosphere above us and shut the gates over us to the 1st and 2nd heaven that has released this spirit over us. And we thank you Lord that this spirit will be replaced with your love, your peace, your forgiveness, and your joy.

Now we need to come together as one voice and release a sound that will cause the **REVOLUTION** to begin in our state and spread throughout this nation!

Chapter 6

Spiritual Identity Theft

John 10:10
The thief does come except to steal, and to kill, and to destroy. I have come that they may have life and that they may have it more abundantly. (NKJ)

We are living in an information and technology world. As we become more and more sophisticated in technology, it seems that criminal activity becomes more sophisticated. Things are happening in the natural realm (things we can see). The natural realm is a place where we can see, feel, and touch things. Also, things continue to happen in the spiritual realm – a place we may not always see what's happening behind the scenes, yet it's going on.

The thing that has been happening in the natural realm has been called "Identity Theft," and I have termed it in the spiritual realm as "Spiritual Identity Theft."

We will be looking at three things regarding Spiritual Identity Theft. What is Identity Theft? What is Spiritual Identity Theft? God wants to restore your Identity and give you an abundant life.

John 10:10
The thief does come except to steal, and to kill, and to destroy. I have come that they may have life and that they may have it more abundantly.

This Scripture says it all.

Before we can discuss Identity Theft we must first understand the word Identity.

The word **Identity** means "the condition of being oneself or itself, and not another; the condition or character as to who a person or what a thing is; the sense of self, providing sameness or continuity in personality over time. (*Webster*)

Another definition might be "the collective aspect of the set of characteristics by which a thing is definitively recognizable or known."

Your identity is what makes you - you! It's how you look, how you speak, how you act, how you make decisions, and how you talk. It's your character.

There is only one you. You may look like some of your relatives, but even though you look like them you may not act like them. You are the only you there is and God knew what He was doing when He created you. It doesn't matter how you got here, or who your mother or father is, God created you the way you are.

There are not two people alike and there are no two finger prints alike.

Identity theft occurs when someone uses your personal identifying information, like your name, social security number or credit card number without your permission to commit fraud or other crimes. The Federal Trade Commission (FTC) estimates that as many as 9 million Americans have their identities stolen each year. In fact, you or someone you know may have experienced some form of identity theft.

The crime takes many forms. Identity thieves may rent an apartment, obtain a credit card, or establish a telephone account in your name. You may not find out about the theft until you review your credit report or a credit card statement and notice charges you didn't make—or until you are contacted by a debt collector.

Identity theft is a serious problem. While some identity theft victims can resolve their problems quickly, others spend hundreds of dollars and many days repairing damage to their good name and credit record. Some consumers victimized by identity theft may lose out on job opportunities, or be denied loans for education, housing or cars because of negative information on their credit reports. In rare cases, they may even be arrested for crimes they did not commit.

Skilled identity thieves may use a variety of methods to get hold of your information, including dumpster diving as when someone rummages through trash looking for bills or other paper with your personal information on it. Skimming is another method used when someone steals your credit/debit card numbers by using a special storage device when processing your card. Phishing is when someone pretends to be a financial institution or company and they send spam or pop-up messages to get you to reveal your personal information.

Your identity can be stolen by changing your address. They divert your billing statements to another location by completing a change of address form. Old-fashioned stealing is when someone steals wallets and purses or mail, including bank and credit card statements; pre-approved credit offers; and new checks or tax information. They steal personnel records, or bribe employees who have access. And finally, pretexting is when someone uses false pretenses to obtain your personal information from financial institutions, telephone companies, and other sources.

Once they have your personal information, identity thieves use it in a variety of ways.

-They may open new credit card accounts in your name. When they use the cards and don't pay the bills, the delinquent accounts appear on your credit report.

-They may change the billing address on your credit card so that you no longer receive bills, and then run up charges on your account. Because your bills are now sent to a different address, it may be some time before you realize there's a problem.

-They may open a new phone or wireless account in your name, or run up charges on your existing account.

-They may use your name to get utility services like electricity, heating, or cable TV.

-They may create counterfeit checks using your name or account number.

-They may open a bank account in your name and write bad checks.

-They may clone your ATM or debit card and make electronic withdrawals in your name, draining your accounts.

-They may take out a loan in your name.

-They may get a driver's license or official ID card issued in your name but with their picture.

-They may use your name and Social Security number to get government benefits.

-They may file a fraudulent tax return using your information.

-They may get a job using your Social Security number.

-They may rent a house or get medical services using your name.

-They may give your personal information to police during an arrest. If they don't show up for their court date, a warrant for arrest is issued in your name.

The best way to find out is to monitor your accounts and

bank statements each month, and check your credit report on a regular basis. If you check your credit report regularly, you may be able to limit the damage caused by identity theft.

Unfortunately, many consumers learn that their identity has been stolen after some damage has already been done.

You may find out when bill collection agencies contact you for overdue debts you never incurred. You may find out when you apply for a mortgage or car loan and learn that problems with your credit history are holding up the loan.

You may find out when you get something in the mail about an apartment you never rented, a house you never bought, or a job you never held.

If you find out that your identity has been stolen you must file a police report, check your credit reports, notify creditors, and dispute any unauthorized transactions. These are some of the steps you must take immediately to restore your good name. It's difficult to predict how long the effects of identity theft may linger. That's because it depends on many factors, including the type of theft, whether the thief sold or passed your information on to other thieves, whether the thief is caught, and problems related to correcting your credit report.

Victims of identity theft should monitor financial records for several months after they discover the crime. Victims should review their credit reports once every three months in the first year of the theft, and once a year thereafter. Stay alert for other signs of identity theft. A great deal of awareness is an effective weapon against many forms of identity theft. Be aware of how information is stolen and what you can do to protect yours, monitor your personal information to uncover any problems quickly, and know what to do when you suspect your identity has been stolen. Armed with the knowledge of how to protect yourself and take action, you can make identity thieves' jobs much more difficult. You can also help fight identity theft by educating your friends, family, and members of your community.

What is Spiritual Identity Theft?

The Bible says in Psalm 139:14, *"I will praise thee; for I am fearfully [and] wonderfully made: marvelous [are] thy works; and [that] my soul knoweth right well. I will praise You, for I am fearfully and wonderfully made; Marvelous are Your works, And that my soul knows very well."*

God said in Gen 1:26, *"Let's make man in our own image."*

Image means physical likeness or representation of a person, form or appearance, according to *Webster*. We were created to look and act like God and to have God's characteristics.

Who is **us**, in this statement from God/ Us is (represents) God the Father, God the Son and God the Holy Spirit. Some of the characteristics of God are;

- ✡ He is a God of love.
- ✡ He is a God of peace.
- ✡ He is a God of joy,
- ✡ He is a God mercy.
- ✡ He is a God of truth.
- ✡ He is a God of goodness.
- ✡ He is a God of justice.
- ✡ He is a God righteousness
- ✡ He is a giving God.

And much more.

Jesus has all these characteristics and more.

Galatians 5:22 tells us, *"But the fruit of the Spirit is love, joy, peace, longsuffering, kindness, goodness, faithfulness, gentleness, self-control. Against such there is no law."* We are to walk in those same characteristics.

Remember it was because of God's love that He sent Jesus to the earth. (**John 3:16**) *"For God so loved the world that He gave His only begotten Son, that whoever believes in Him should not perish but have everlasting life."* Jesus came as a man of destiny and purpose. We should be like Him we should have the same characteristics and we should be people of destiny.

(Luke 4:18)

18) *"The Spirit of the LORD is upon Me, Because He has anointed Me to preach the gospel to the poor; He has sent Me to heal the brokenhearted, To proclaim liberty to the captives and recovery of sight to the blind,*

To set at liberty those who are oppressed;

19) "To proclaim the acceptable year of the LORD."

✝ He came to do God's will. (John 6:38)

✝ He came to save sinners (Luke 19:10)

✝ He came to destroy the works of the enemy (I John 3:8)

And much more…

We are to be like Him, people on a mission to do the will of God the Father. Jesus said, "My meat is to do the will of Him who sent me." In **Jeremiah 1:5 it says,** *"Before I formed you in the womb I knew you; before you were born I sanctified you; I ordained you a prophet to the nations."*

God is saying here before you were born I had already "set you apart" from everybody else for a work for me. I had placed an assignment beside your name. God says *"I had appointed you to be a prophet to the nations,"* He is saying I already knew what I wanted you to do. I had already given you dreams and visions for your life. I've already put in your heart my desires for your life.

In Romans 8:29-30 it says, *"For whom He foreknew, He also predestined to be conformed to the image of His Son, that He might be the firstborn among many brethren.*

Moreover whom He predestined, these He also called; whom He called, these He also justified; and whom He justified, and these He also glorified."

Foreknew (knew you before birth)

Pre- (means before)

Destine (means to be set apart for a particular use, purpose, or intent). (*Webster*)

So He had already set you apart for a particular use, purpose, or intent before your momma had you), to be conformed to the image of His Son, that He might be the firstborn among many brethren. So you are no accident or incident you were born with an assignment, you were born with a purpose; you were born with intent from God. But something happened along the way.

Because of major atrocities that man has aloud the enemy to do to other men there has been much abuse in this world. When Abraham sent his sons away many things happened to their soul. Many wars with other nations and each other took place in the African culture. This book by no means is saying that the African people are the only group of people that has suffered a major atrocity. The Jews had the Holocaust, the Native Americans had their Trail of Tears, China had Lushan Rebellion in 18th century, Indians had the Thuggee sect, and `the Africans had slavery. In a period of 400 years, between 150 to 600 million black Africans died. Those who survived were better off dead. They were treated worse than animals. Tortured, raped and mutilated, they had no meaningful existence at all. The Africans lost their culture, their language, their will, their pride, and even today the social effects of African slavery can still be seen all around the world.

The slaves were brainwashed. It is said that step one to brainwashing is to work at people's most fundamental awareness. Shape them at the neurological level so they develop the faculties to take your input and call it "thinking for myself." Enable them to stop thinking.

One of the tactics whites used to oppress slaves was destroying families. Over time, broken families became normal to blacks. Many believe that black families are just naturally dysfunctional. They think that it's in a black man's DNA to have multiple baby mamas or to abandon his family; that it's a black woman's birthright to distrust men, to gold dig, and to undermine a man's role in the home. The truth is that slave traders/owners went to extremes to make sure we never had a chance to practice and cultivate strong nuclear families or pass on that tradition to our children. The portrayal of blacks as sex objects is tied to the portrayal of blacks as savages and beasts. Historical brainwashing efforts likened the sexual activity of blacks to those of animals—purely carnal with no emotions, sentiment, affection, or love. During slavery blacks learned that sex was power. In a society that deemed them powerless, they could use sex to get what they wanted. The same is true today with the video girls and strippers who claim that they're just making money, as if there are no other ways to make money. For men, who have historically been labeled "boy," sex was seen as the only way to assert their manhood. So this one's for all the over sexed rappers and video vixens, and everyone who supports and celebrates them. What we should understand is that we have the power to attain power without debasing ourselves as sex objects with no dignity. Another manifestation of brainwashing is rampant, but like all the others, it's seen as normal. People get angry (really angry) when you suggest that perhaps their preference for white, mixed, or fair skinned people may be a product of a white superiority/black inferiority complex. Black people learned to associate their unhappy lives, oppression, slave status, second class citizenship, etc. with their skin color, hair texture, and facial features. Blacks are dying at alarming rates from diseases that are preventable and curable, such as diabetes, heart disease, and stress. This goes back to slavery brainwashing that we are not valuable so why do we need to take care of ourselves. One of the reasons that African-Americans spend all their money on superficial things is more than just materialism – it's brainwashing. In a world that promotes African-American inferiority, blacks feel the need to prove themselves, to perpetrate, to validate, to feel and show themselves worthy. But we're working at this from the wrong end. We need to start by building wealth in our hearts and minds, then building actual monetary wealth for our families and communities. We were taught not to expect high academic performance from African-Americans. Before the slave trade even began in America, Europeans depicted Africans as inferior. But it's not just entertainment media that portrays this, it's so called scientific and academic media. In the book *Brain Washed*, Burrell quotes: Many prominent biologists, sociologists, psychologists, and anthropologists dedicated their scholarly lives to proving the moral and intellectual inferiority of Africans and their descendants to justify the racism endemic in U.S. institutions.

Many African-Americans have been taught (brainwashed) to be passive as though they have no control of their lives and they must accept their situation until an outside power changes it for them. We wait for saviors to show us the way out and tell us what to do and think. Because of brainwashing, some African-Americans don't really believe they have control of their lives.

With this being said African-Americans have been victims of spiritual identity theft. We have not known our place in God's Kingdom. We were taught that not only were we inferior in the world but when it came to Jehovah God we were presented with a picture of a white face blue-eyed Jesus who looked at us as animals and who thought we were second class citizens. When taught the gospel there were some who caught the message that God loved us just as we were and that He was our Savior. Praise God for those who kept the faith, it is because of their prayers that today the African-American, African and many other cultures are having their identity restored.

We have found out that God is the Lord of all people. He is an equal opportunity employer. He is no respecter of persons. We have found out that we are the seed of Abraham, Isaac, and Jacob and we have a heritage just like any other culture. It is time for African-American people to understand their heritage in Jesus Christ and to come into His kingdom and serve the Lord of lords and the King of kings. I believe that every culture has a redemptive heritage in the Kingdom. I believe that culture has a part to play in ushering our King back at His second coming and that as the Word says all things work together for good to those who love the Lord and to those that are called according to His purpose. I'm reminded of how Joseph's brothers sold him into slavery because of jealousy and later his life was used to save a nation of people. Could it be that the African-American people have suffered through slavery and many other harsh things in order for God to use them in this end time to save nations? Whatever the enemy means for our evil, God has a wonderful way of turning it around for our good. Could this be one of those situations? It is very possible according to some of the prophetic words you will see in Chapter Nine. God wants everyone to understand who they are and who He has created them to be. Everyone has a purpose and a destiny that needs fulfilling. As we continue to follow God's Word and obey His commands I believe more revelation will come in regards to who the African people really are and their role in God's Kingdom.

Chapter 7

An Orphan Spirit

It is estimated there are 210 million orphans worldwide (recent UNICEF report.) The UNICEF orphan numbers DON'T include abandonment (millions of children) as well as sold and/or trafficked children. The current population of the United States is just a little over 300 million... to give you an idea of the enormity of the numbers...

- 86 million orphans in India
- 44 million orphans in Africa by 2010
- 10 million orphans in Mexico
- 35,000 children die every day from hunger and malnutrition.

According to data released in 2003 as many as eight million boys and girls around the world live in institutional care. Some studies have found that violence in residential institutions is six times higher than violence in foster care, and that children in group care are almost four times more likely to experience sexual abuse than children in family based care.

-Every day 5,760 more children become orphans

-Approximately 250,000 children are adopted annually, but...

-Each year 14, 505, 000 children grow up as orphans and age out of the system by age sixteen

-Each day 38,493 orphans age out

-Every 2.2 seconds another orphan ages out with no family to belong to and no place to call home

Studies have shown that 10% – 15% of these children commit suicide before they reach age 18

These studies also show that 60% of the girls become prostitutes and 70% of the boys become hardened criminals.

Another study reported that of the 15,000 orphans aging out of state-run institutions every year, 10% committed suicide, 5,000 were unemployed, 6,000 were homeless and 3,000 were in prison within three years...

An estimated 1.2 million children are trafficked every year; (THE STATE OF THE WORLD'S CHILDREN, 2005)

2 million children, the majority of them girls, are sexually exploited in the multibillion-dollar commercial sex industry. (THE STATE OF THE WORLD'S CHILDREN, 2005)

- By 2015 it is projected that there will be 400 million orphaned children worldwide.
- HIV/AIDS alone has orphaned 15 million children, most of them in Sub-Saharan Africa.
- In the countries of Central and Eastern Europe and Central Asia, a total of 1.3 million children live in institutional care.

USA Facts and Statistics:

In the U.S., 423,000 children are living without permanent families in the foster care system.

115,000 of these children are eligible for adoption, but nearly 40% of these children will wait over three years in foster care before being adopted.

Around the world, there are an estimated 163 million orphans who have lost one parent. There are 13 million orphans who have lost both parents and are living in orphanages or on the streets and lack the care and attention required for healthy development. These children are at risk for disease, malnutrition, and death.

U.S. families adopted more than 12,700 children through intercountry adoption in fiscal year 2009.

China is the top sending country, followed by Ethiopia, Russia, South Korea, and Guatemala.

Intercountry adoption has been on the decline since its peak in 2004 at 22,990 adoptions.

No child under three years of age should be placed in institutional care without a parent or primary caregiver. This is based on results from 32 European countries, including nine in-depth country studies, which considered the "risk of harm in terms of attachment disorder, developmental delay and neural atrophy in the developing brain."

Children raised in orphanages have an IQ 20 points lower than their peers in foster care, according to a meta-analysis of 75 studies (more than 3,800 children in 19 countries). This shows the need for children to be raised in families, not in institutions. Each year, over 29,000 youth "age out" of foster care without the emotional and financial support necessary to succeed. This number has steadily risen over the past decade. Nearly 40% had been homeless or couch surfed, nearly 60% of young men had been convicted of a crime, and only 48% were employed. About 75% of women and 33% of men receive government benefits to meet basic needs, and 50% of all youth who aged out were involved in substance use and 17% of the females were pregnant.

Nearly 25% of youth aging out did not have a high school diploma or GED, and a mere 6% had finished a two- or four-year degree after aging out of foster care. One study shows 70% of all youth in foster care have the desire to attend college.

Over 65,000 children in foster care in the U.S. are placed in institutions or group homes, not in traditional foster homes.

Neglect was reported for 54% of all children entering foster care by their parent or primary caregiver. Parental substance abuse was a circumstance present for 28% of the children entering care.

States spent a mere 1.2-1.3% of available federal funds on parent recruitment and training services even though 22% of children in foster care had adoption as their goal. Over three years is the average length of time a child waits to be adopted in foster care. Roughly 55% of these children have had three or more placements. An earlier study found that 33% of children had changed elementary schools five or more times, losing relationships and falling behind educationally.

Adopted children make-up roughly 2% of the total child population under the age of 18, but 11% of all adolescents referred for therapy have been adopted. Post-adoption services are important to all types of adoption, whether foster care adoption, international adoption, or domestic infant adoption, according to the (CCAI) Congressional Coalition on Adoption Institute.

According to The Effects of Early Social-Emotional and Relationship Experience on the Development of Young Orphanage Children, orphans raised in globally deficient orphanages weigh less, have less girth and are shorter than children who are not raised in orphanages. This is due in part to many aspects of their early environment, such as poor nutrition, lack of sufficient physical exercise, and shoddy medical care. Another possible cause is psychosocial dwarfism, a condition that children who are exposed to severe social and emotional neglect become susceptible to when growing up in orphanages.

Orphans living in global deficient orphanages display a delay in behavioral development. Acting out emerges in adolescent orphans whose parents have died from AIDS. Orphans tend to engage in atypical behavior that begins as overly passive and grows to aggressiveness in the teen years. Being easily distracted and overreacting are other behavioral characterizations of orphans living in substandard orphanages. Depression, withdrawal from social activities, moodiness, loss or increased appetite, and sleep problems are common reactions in adolescent orphans who have lost parents to AIDS. Sometimes, alcohol and drug use can be a manifestation of extreme depression in these adolescent orphans.

In Africa, there are 60 million orphaned and vulnerable children (HIV/Aids, conflict, disability, street children). (Worldbank) This is not just an opinion. According to Children-our investment.org, homes without fathers ultimately affect children in numerous tragic ways:

- 63 percent of youth suicides are from fatherless homes
- 90 percent of all homeless and runaway children are from fatherless homes
- 85 percent of all children who show behavior disorders come from fatherless homes
- 80 percent of rapists with anger problems come from fatherless homes
- 71 percent of all high school dropouts come from fatherless homes
- 75 percent of all adolescent patients in chemical-abuse centers come from fatherless homes
- 85 percent of all youths in prison come from fatherless homes

These statistics apply to African-American homes in disproportionate numbers. Compared with the 72 percent in our communities, 17 percent of Asians, 29 percent of whites, 53 percent of Hispanics and 66 percent of Native Americans were born to unwed mothers in 2008, the most recent year for which government figures are available. The rate for the overall U.S. population was 41 percent.

Dealing with an Orphan Spirit

Because of the way Abraham had his sons leave (Keturah's sons) it created a door for many deep emotional hurts to come into their lives. As discussed earlier one would be feeling like an orphan.

"I will not leave you orphans, I will come to you" (John 14:18).

"But you have received the spirit of adoption" (Romans 8:15 c.f Gal. 4:5)

An orphan is someone who had been abandoned by their primary caregiver. The Kingdom of God is based upon relationship, and the central relationship is one of parent to child - father to son. *"Older women. should admonish the younger women"* (Titus 2:4). *"Timothy, my true son in the faith"* (1 Timothy 1:2). *"I am your father in the gospel"* (1 Corinthians 4:15).

We become orphaned when those who are caring for us abandon us, or when those who should care, do not. We may have an orphan spirit because of the natural parenting we received was not correct. Maybe you were literally abandoned, or adopted out. Maybe you had an absent father, or abusive mother. Maybe you raised yourself because of the financial condition of your family, or the number of children in the home. On the spiritual side, neglect happens at every level in institutional Christianity.

Leaders find themselves demanding instead of admonishing and berating instead of beseeching. We are busy with church life instead of the life inside the people, and are being fathered by the system themselves. There are promises of parental love, but in reality, it is rarely seen in the church.

Usual characteristics of an orphan spirit:
- They are unable to have lasting relationships
- They have a strong hatred of authority, general distrust for leaders
- They often have a lack of direction for their lives
- They are unable to make major key strategic decisions
- It is hard for them to have intimacy
- They usually operate in a fear of rejection, inherited rejection, and perceived rejection
- They make sure that they reject others before they can be rejected
- There is a huge fear of failure and they feel as if they never are quite good enough
- There is a drive to be an over achiever, to succeed, win, prove yourself to others
- They are always looking for something bigger and better
- They are usually very unteachable (know everything)
- They bounce around and are unable to stay at one church, always moving from church to church
- They need constant recognition for even some things
- They are easily offended
- They often have feelings of abandonment even when one has not been abandoned
- They have a survivalist mentality always looking out for oneself and not going to let anyone hurt them.

"But you have received the spirit of adoption" (Romans 8:15 and Galatians 4:5)

How to Pray off an Orphan Spirit

As I went back to look at the 1/7/11 Commissioning within the first 15 minutes I saw something I had not seen before – the entire commissioning was based on two things:

1.For me to raise up an army of African-Americans who will stand with Israel.

2.I got anointed to break the orphan spirit off people and nations. When I was in Texas I am finally getting it. Most of my family takes in orphans. As messed up as we have been in the past God still used my mother, my sister and others to take in orphans. So here is something else that Satan did not want me to see. And some of you have the same care.

Malachi 4:6 (NKJV):

And he will turn, The hearts of the fathers to the children,
And the hearts of the children to their fathers,
Lest I come and strike the earth with a curse."

There has to be much prayer for those who have an "orphan spirit". It may be that you feel like you have an orphan spirit and didn't know what it was or that some of these characteristics applied to you. We want to help you get free from this spirit in order for you to be able to relate with others and fulfill your God given destiny. Here's one example of a prayer:

Father you have given Jesus all power to stop the enemy and you have given us all power to stop the enemy from operating in our lives. So I plead the Blood of Jesus upon every person who has any of these characteristics of an orphan spirit and I bind every spirit of an orphan from their lives. I ask the Holy Spirit to hover over them to bring healing and deliverance. I break the power of an orphan spirit from over their hearts, minds, soul and spirit now in the name of Jesus.

Lord, you are their Father and I pray that they will receive the spirit of adoption (Romans 8:15) whereby we cry Abba father and that they will call You, "Abba." Lord I pray that healing will come to every area of their hearts, minds, spirit and souls. Where their hearts have become stony and hard, I pray that you would make it a heart of flesh (Ezekiel 11:19).

Lord, I ask that you will bring godly, loving, committed spiritual fathers into their lives that they will receive and honor, and to cover them in prayer, to give them direction and to love them. God, please help these spiritual fathers to have the mind and heart of Christ and to understand this person. In Jeremiah 3:19 it says, *"But I said: 'How can I put you among the children And give you a pleasant land, A beautiful heritage of the hosts of nations?' "And I said: 'You shall call Me, "My Father," And not turn away from Me.'*

The scripture of Jeremiah 3:15 reveals, *"And I will give you shepherds according to My heart, who will feed you with knowledge and understanding. So Father God give unto them spiritual fathers who will be godly shepherds to them according to Your heart and will feed them with Your knowledge and Your understanding. In Jesus name, Amen."*

These prayers are a good way to start helping these people to start embracing deliverance and healing in this area and to begin allowing the Holy Spirit to soften their hearts.

The following prayer is for them to pray daily until breakthrough comes:

Jesus, I ask You to please forgive me for feeling like an orphan and embracing the attitudes, actions and heart of an orphan. Your desire for me is that I am a healthy part of a godly spiritual family. I break all soul ties that have formed with the enemy and I have formed with an orphan spirit, rejection, fear, unforgiveness and all spirits that have come in as a result of feeling abandoned in Jesus name.

I command all my members, my body, heart, mind and spirit to align with God's will and purpose for me, in Jesus name. Lord, I ask that you would heal my mind, soul, spirit and my heart from the spirits of abandonment, separation, rejection and fatherlessness.

God please help me to have the heart of a son and please help me to turn my heart toward my spiritual father. Lord, please help me to pray for, see the need, support, and understand the spiritual fathers you have placed in my life.

Please help me to have the attitude and heart that Jesus had toward You as a Father when He walked this earth. Lord, please reveal to me all areas in my life that have been wounded, hurt, discouraged and disappointed.

Please heal all those areas in my life and make me whole. Lord I ask that you would help me to forgive and release everyone who I looked to as a spiritual father or leader who wounded me or failed me in the past. Lord, please help me to commit to the church and spiritual father that You have strategically selected for me to be with. In Jesus' Name, Amen.

If you are called to be a spiritual father...then never, never, never give up.

Chapter 8

God's Healing & Restoration

We are so thankful that God is a God of restoration. He wants to restore every one of us to the original intent He had for us and our destiny from the beginning.

When you study the history of Africa and African people you will find that they were deep into idolatry. They worshipped all types of gods and did all types of abominations in their worship. I believe this is where slavery and many other things were allowed to enter in against Africa and its people. Today many of these practices still exist and the people and land are still suffering. The Bible says a curse without a cause will not alight.

In Proverbs 26:2 it reads, *"Like a flitting sparrow, like a flying swallow, So a curse without cause shall not alight."*

Remember the story of David and the Gibeonites; 2 Samuel 21:1-6, *"There was a famine during David's reign that lasted for three years, so David asked the LORD about it. And the LORD said, "The famine has come because Saul and his family are guilty of murdering the Gibeonites." 2) So King David summoned the Gibeonites. They were not part of Israel but were all that was left of the nation of the Amorites. Israel had sworn not to kill them, but Saul, in his zeal, had tried to wipe them out. 3) David asked them, "What can I do for you to make amends? Tell me so that the*

LORD *will bless his people again." 4) "Well, money won't do it,"* *the Gibeonites replied. "And we don't want to see the Israelites* *executed in revenge." "What can I do then?" David asked. "Just* *tell me and I will do it for you." 5) Then they replied, "It was Saul* *who planned to destroy us, to keep us from having any place at all* *in Israel. 6) So let seven of Saul's sons or grandsons be handed over* *to us, and we will execute them before the LORD at Gibeon, on the* *mountain of the LORD. "All right," the king said, "I will do it."*

David had to do something to amend what had been done to the Gibeonites. Thank God today that we don't go around killing people for things like this because I might not be around because of something my parents or grandparents did. Today we have forgiveness of sins through Jesus Christ's death on the cross, according to 1 John 1:9 which says *"If we confess our sins, He is faithful and just to forgive us of our sins, and cleanses us from all unrighteousness."* There are also times we must go back and repay in whatever way God tells us to and make some situations right. There are many movements that are helping restore the Native Americans by giving them land, money, and education. The Japanese received restoration for what was done to them in "Nearly 20 years ago, Congress did apologize for the treatment of Japanese Americans who were imprisoned in internment camps during World War II and paid each person $20,000." I'm not sure what should be given back because this thing goes so deep and has done so much damage, but our creator God knows and all we have to do is listen to Him and He will show us how to correct this evil that the enemy has done to African-American and Hispanic people. (SeTe Appendix 1 Apologies).

The Bible has much to say about things that have been lost and/or stolen and how God wants to restore them. Restore means to give back.

re•store, re•stored, re•stor•ing.

1. To bring back into existence, use, or the like; reestablish: to restore order.
2. to bring back to a former, original, or normal condition, as a building, statue, or painting.
3. to bring back to a state of health, soundness, or vigor.
4. to put back to a former place, or to a former position, rank, etc.: to restore the king to his throne.
5. to give back; make return or restitution of (anything taken away or lost). (Dictionary.com)

Exodus 22:1 - *"If a man steals an ox or a sheep, and slaughters it or sells it, he shall restore five oxen for an ox and four sheep for a sheep."*

Exodus 22:4 - *"If the theft is certainly found alive in his hand, whether it is an ox or donkey or sheep, he shall restore double."*

2 Samuel 12:6 - *"And he shall restore fourfold for the lamb, because he did this thing and because he had no pity."*

Leviticus 6:4 - *"then it shall be, because he has sinned and is guilty, that he shall restore what he has stolen, or the thing which he has extorted, or what was delivered to him for safekeeping, or the lost thing which he found"*

Leviticus 6:5 - *"or all that about which he has sworn falsely. He shall restore its full value, add one-fifth more to it, [and] give it to whomever it belongs, on the day of his trespass offering."*

Land

Judges 11:13 – *"And the king of the people of Ammon answered the messengers of Jephthah, "Because Israel took away my land when they came up out of Egypt, from the Arnon as far as the Jabbok, and to the Jordan. Now therefore, **restore those** [lands] peaceably."*

2 Samuel 9:7 – *"So David said to him, "Do not fear, for I will surely show you kindness for Jonathan your father's sake, and will **restore** to you all the land of Saul your grandfather; and you shall eat bread at my table continually."*

Cities and businesses

1 Kings 20:34 – *"So [Ben-Hadad] said to him, "The cities which my father took from your father I will **restore;** and you may set up marketplaces for yourself in Damascus, as my father did in Samaria." Then [Ahab said], "I will send you away with this treaty." So he made a treaty with him and sent him away.*

2 Kings 8:6 – *"And when the king asked the woman, she told him. So the king appointed a certain officer for her, saying, **"Restore all that** [was] hers, and all the proceeds of the field from the day that she left the land until now."*

Nehemiah 5:11 - **"Restore now to them,** *even this day, their lands, their vineyards, their olive groves, and their houses, also a hundredth of the money and the grain, the new wine and the oil, that you have charged them."*

Nehemiah 5:12 – *"So they said, "We will **restore** [it], and will require nothing from them; we will do as you say." Then I called the priests, and required an oath from them that they would do according to this promise."*

I travel throughout the U.S. and abroad preaching and teaching on various subjects. One of my teachings deals with

Proverbs 13:22 that says, *"the wealth of the wicked is laid up for the just"*. This means that at some point the Bible is saying that there is going to be a massive wealth transference to God's people. As I travel, usually I'll ask my host to give me a tour of the city and some history (I would have already done some research to understand what is operating in that city). It seems like it never fails that they will show me an area where African-Americans would have had businesses, shops, stores, banks etc… and would have been flourishing at one time and for some reason the cities or counties plans/laws or violence would come along and put them out of business. For example, Black Wall Street may refer to: Greenwood, Tulsa, Oklahoma, the area of northeast Oklahoma around Tulsa, home to several prominent black businessmen. In 1921, Greenwood, a successful all-black enclave in Tulsa, was the site of the deadliest race riot in U.S. history.

Jackson Ward, a thriving African-American business community in Richmond, Virginia, was once thriving and declined due to desegregation. Along with other communities, including Parrish Street in Durham, North Carolina, also an area of successful black-owned businesses.

With all this being said God wants to restore these things that have been lost and stolen. If you'll go to the Appendix of this book you will see a list of federal and state governments, businesses, and religious organizations who have apologized for slavery. This is a very good start to restoration, but more has to be done. (See Economics of Slavery)

Psalms 51:12 – *"**Restore** to me the joy of Your salvation, And uphold me [by Your] generous Spirit."*

Psalms 80:3 – *"**Restore us**, O God; Cause Your face to shine, And we shall be saved!"*

Psalms 80:7 – *"**Restore us**, O God of hosts; Cause Your face to shine, And we shall be saved!"*

Psalms 80:19 – *"**Restore us**, O LORD God of hosts; Cause Your face to shine, And we shall be saved!"*

Psalms 85:4 – *"**Restore us**, O God of our salvation, And cause Your anger toward us to cease."*

Proverbs 6:30 – *"[People] do not despise a thief If he steals to satisfy himself when he is starving."*

Proverbs 6:31 – *"Yet [when] he is found, he must **restore** sevenfold; He may have to give up all the substance of his house."*

People in the United States want to act as if slavery didn't happen, but it did. I believe when we really hear how God wants us to reconcile around this issue, that is when the thief has really been exposed (Satan) and then every one of us will be restored.

I believe that some of the laws that are being passed in this nation are because we haven't fully dealt with our own hearts around slavery and issues that are still happening in this area. The Bible says (I repeat) a curse without a cause will not alight. Proverbs 26:2 says, *"Like a flitting sparrow, like a flying swallow, So a curse without cause shall not alight."* I believe once the church deals with its real feelings around slavery, on both sides, (African Americans & Caucasian Americans) our nation will become truly FREE!

Here are some things God wants to restore to the African-American and Hispanic people.

Righteous Judges and Cities

Isaiah 1:26 – *"I will restore your judges as at the first, And your counselors as at the beginning. Afterward you shall be called the city of righteousness, the faithful city."*

Life

Isaiah 38:16 – *"O Lord, by these [things men] live; And in all these [things is] the life of my spirit; So You will restore me and make me live."*

Lamentations 1:11 – *"All her people sigh, They seek bread; They have given their valuables for food to restore life."See, O LORD, and consider, For I am scorned."*

To Their Place

Jeremiah 27:22 – *"They shall be carried to Babylon, and there they shall be until the day that I visit them,' says the LORD. 'Then I will bring them up and restore them to this place".*

Health

Jeremiah 30:17 – *"For I will restore health to you And heal you of your wounds,' says the LORD, 'Because they called you an outcast [saying]: "This [is] Zion; No one seeks her."*

Isaiah 57:18 – *"I have seen his ways, and will heal him; I will also lead him, And restore comforts to him And to his mourners."*

Time

Joel 2:25 - *"So I will restore to you the years that the swarming locust has eaten, The crawling locust, The consuming locust, And the chewing locust, My great army which I sent among you."*

Excellence

Nahum 2:2 – *"For the LORD will restore the excellence of Jacob, Like the excellence of Israel, For the emptiers have emptied them out, And ruined their vine branches."*

Pure Language

Zephaniah 3:9 - *"For then I will restore to the peoples a pure language, That they all may call on the name of the LORD, To serve Him with one accord".*

Double

Zechariah 9:12 – *"Return to the stronghold, You prisoners of hope. Even today I declare [That] I will restore double to you."*

All things

Matthew 17:11 – *"Jesus answered and said to them, "Indeed, Elijah is coming first and will restore all things."*

The Kingdom

Act 1:6 – *"Therefore, when they had come together, they asked Him, saying, "Lord, will You at this time restore the kingdom to Israel?"*

People

Galatians 6:1 – *"Brethren, if a man is overtaken in any trespass, you who [are] spiritual restore such a one in a spirit of gentleness, considering yourself lest you also be tempted."*

There must be a Payback

Luke 19:8 – *"Then Zacchaeus stood and said to the Lord, "Look, Lord, I give half of my goods to the poor; and if I have taken anything from anyone by false accusation, I restore fourfold."*

Is there no one to cry restore!

Isaiah 42:1 - *"Behold! My Servant whom I uphold, My Elect One [in whom] My soul delights! I have put My Spirit upon Him;*

He will bring forth justice to the Gentiles."

Isaiah 42:4 – *"He will not fail nor be discouraged, Till He has established justice in the earth; And the coastlands shall wait for His law."*

Isaiah 42:22 – *"But this [is] a people robbed and plundered; All of them are snared in holes, And they are hidden in prison houses; They are for prey, and no one delivers; For plunder, and no one says, **"Restore!"***

I guess I could sum up the purpose of this book in this section. I have been called by God to cry out restore for these two people groups who have lost much and have not had God's full restoration to come into their lives.

The Bible say the gift of prophecy edifies, exhorts, and comforts (I Corinthians 14:3); helps us build up or strengthen; and should lead us to the Word of God. It is the ministry of the Holy Spirit to convict of sin, of righteousness, and of judgment to come (John 16:8-11). A person can use their intellect, faith, and will as an operative in this gift, but its exercise is not intellectually based. It is calling forth words from the Spirit of God. The gift of prophecy operates when there is high worship (I Samuel 10:5-6), when others' prophets are present (I Samuel 10:9-10), and when hands are laid on you by ministers (Acts 19:1-6). Prophecy helps give a person direction and encourages them in some cases to go forward to do all that God has called them to do.

I have received permission from some of the well-known national and international prophets who have given prophetic words regarding African-American people destiny and would like to share them with you. This will give us all a better understanding of who God has called the African-American and African people to be in these end-times.

Chapter 9

Prophetic Words

In this chapter I would like to share some of the prophetic words given by some of the most powerful national and international prophetic voices around the world in regards to African-Americans.

Pastor Tony Cavener
Black Gold (First Published In 1996)

As a son of Oklahoma and Texas I grew up hearing oil referred to as "black gold." The "black gold" of oil in Oklahoma and Texas was the source of those two states' greatest wealth. I believe our Lord has also deposited a great wealth in our nation, a glorious deposit of "Black Gold"- black men and women who will be the "oil" in the cities of America who will fuel revival as the Lord's fire falls in our land.

The Lord gave me a picture of His hand gathering and preserving for Himself a remnant of "Black Gold" from Islamic Africa more than 300 years ago....this remnant became acquainted with the "fellowship of His sufferings" and knew the lash and of slavery. In their affliction they sowed fields in America that, when ripe, would be "White for the Harvest," (in the natural fields of cotton).

Through their affliction they developed a rich history of faith in Christ, they were gifted with rich songs of hope, and a dignity born out of trial and suffering. They saw a history of emancipation in the 1860's and liberation in the 1960's with the emergence of a gifted and prophetic leader in the Reverend Dr. Martin Luther King. No matter how modern church historians record his life, he truly was a man raised up by God for a crucial hour in the history of this nation.

Now, 30 years later, it is time for us to intercede and pray for God to raise up the anointed, broken, humble, and gifted black men and women who, through His hand, will ignite the "Black Gold" in the cities of America!

A Wind of Mercy

We have seen the "Black Gold" ignited by the enemy through the torch of hatred, agony, and prejudice, when we watched Los Angeles burn with hatred after the Rodney King trial in the early 1990s. A wind of mercy blew from the throne of God with a "not guilty" verdict in the O.J. trial. Regardless of anyone's opinion (and that's what they are, for there is only one Judge, and we should leave judgment in His eternal hands), God had mercy on this nation and kept the fires of "hatred" at bay!

Time to Intercede!

Let's seize the window of opportunity that the Lord has graciously handed us and pray for the fire of God's revival to ignite the precious "Black Gold" that He deposited in this country more than 300 years ago. Some precious people, white and black, have been called to leave all and pour out their lives in caring for the poor of the inner cities but they tend to be in the minority. However, the black community as a whole is still unimpacted and I believe will be until we repent of our arrogance and pride. We must stop seeing the white church as the equippers of the blacks and cry out in prayer and intercession for the Lord himself to raise up anointed black men and women to be leaders and equippers of the church. Broken, humble black leaders filled with His Spirit and a passion for Christ, must rise up and demonstrate compassion for their people, love for His church, and a fervent hope for revival for all the people of this Nation!

I believe as this takes place we will see the precious "Black Gold" deposited by the Lord in this country ignite throughout cities across America with passionate flames of revival in a way this world has never seen! At the beginning of this century, we saw the flames of "Pentecostal revival" break out in Los Angeles at a place called Azusa Street in meetings led by humble, anointed "black leaders", and from this Azusa Street Revival was birthed the great Pentecostal Denominations we know today as well as the Charismatic Renewal! I believe it is in God's heart to see at the end of this century the flames of an even greater "Pentecostal revival" burn as the "Black Gold" of this nation catches fire for God. Just as at the beginning of this century the "Black Gold" ignited the whole church in revival fire so we are poised now for the torch of God's passion to ignite the "Black Gold" again!

As the black forefathers of our nation planted and sowed with tears and suffering the fields of white in this land centuries ago, and our black "mothers" wept over their own children of which they were bereaved, and loved and nurtured the children, not their own, entrusted to their care. Let us pray that their heirs will reap in joy the spiritual fields that are even now "white unto harvest," and nurture and bring forth in mighty revival the children who are spiritual heirs to the Kingdom of God in this nation of ours.

Our Posture in This Hour

Let us continue to receive with great joy and passion the Lord's gracious outpouring of renewal, yet at the same time let us assume a posture of humility and repentance for our arrogance, pride, and fear and recognize that as a nation we were built on the foundations of both "black and white." As the church in this nation we will see revival only as we accept that we as "black and white" brothers and sisters are "joint heirs to the promises of God" one "new man in Christ" and indeed are co-laborers in the fields of harvest together as equals in the Kingdom of God!

Prophet Chuck Pierce (2000)

He had all the African-Americans stand up at a particular service in the Atlanta, Georgia area and pronounced a Joseph anointing on them.

Prophet Chuck Pierce (2001 in Oklahoma City)

"I just say go forth in prayer, for I will supernaturally orchestrate a gathering of black men and black women throughout this nation into Tulsa. And I say it will change the religious structure of this land," saith the Lord.

Joseph Ginat (Oklahoma City)

"I would say to you because you have welcomed covenant into your midst. I will now over turn the racial riots that have plagued this particular land", saith the Lord. "I say there will be new churches to arise and I say Afro-Americans will begin to go forth, and I say there will be a great release of Afro-Americans throughout this state," said the Lord.

Prophet Chuck Pierce (June 2005)

We were on a financial prayer journey in New York. At dinner that night there were six of us. Prophetic Chuck looked at me and began speaking prophetically. He said the African-Americans will be the next group to rise up. If you don't go into a religious structure or put color before the gospel you will cause this nation to do well. But if you go into a religious structure and put color before the gospel you will cause this nation to be lost. You don't have to try and take anything, God has given you leadership. You have the Joseph anointing.

Prophet Chuck Pierce (October 2005)

He gave to an African-American woman at Zion Ministries. And the Lord would say to you daughter "I have held your people for a time such as this. There is a Joseph anointing within them that will begin to be released right now. For they have a sound of victory in the midst of war, for they had to harden themselves to circumstances. Even now there is much confusion and much realignment needed and I will deal with it, for this could be a people that could go astray at this time."

Chuck Pierce Summary (African-American Prophecy Oct. 2, 2006)

Atlanta is, I believe – well, based on what the Lord said last night, is more than I can comprehend.

This is what I saw: I saw Him go blow on the root of revolution, where revolution started in our nation up north. You can go back and look at some of those revolutionary places that occurred in the northern part of our nation that produced a revolution of freedom in this country. I saw the Lord blow on that, but He said; "now I'm going to blow the seeds of revolution south." And I saw this area becoming the *headquarters of a major revolution* that would change the course of this nation. I don't know exactly how to define the aspect of that revolution yet, on what's going to be here, but it was very clear. **When it hit Atlanta it mingled with the seeds of revolution of the Civil Rights Movement.** The phase of it that began 40 years ago came to an end this past February. Now this will create a whole new type of movement that causes our nation to go in the direction of its future.

... I believe we are at that place in these next two years. **I see Black America rising up and leading our nation and with that, that is going to create a revolution.** But it's going to create a revolution in a different way than we think because what will happen is the cultures of Black America will clash. Now hear me. That's where the clash is going to come. It will be a religious clash in the midst of the Black culture and we will have to choose how we align with that clash. It is almost like you will have to bring us into war with you, I'm speaking to Black America and its leadership. And that is how our nation will begin to take its course for the future. Because we still have not come into the concept of the religious war we are involved in. We've got to see lots of changes come. I don't even want to call it a religious war, we're in a "covenant war" – that's what God said in October 2000, that we would be in war by September 18, 2001, and it would be a covenant war and the first hit would come on New York City. The reason this could be so accurately prophesied was because there were more Jews in New York City at that time than in Israel.

Kim Clement (December 30, 2006)

God says, "In the death of the **grandfather of soul**, a nation, a generation of **African-Americans, shall rise up**, and they shall preach; they shall preach with a style that has never been heard before. They shall be the perpetrators and the creators of a brand new **soul spirit sound**, that shall reach the unreachable and touch the untouchable," says the Lord of Hosts.

Prophetic Vision

By profession I serve as a career advisor and trainer contractor for three counties - Barrow, Jackson, and- Walton in [where?]. My clients are TANF recipients. In the last two months more than half of my classes have been pregnant women. Some of the young women were at different stages: eight months, six, five or three months. As I was praying, the Lord showed me a vision that most of the people coming to be a part of this movement are pregnant with this vision or various parts. Some are ready to go into labor while others are just starting. He said it is going to be like a maternity ward when various ones come together. But each had some role to play.

Based on these prophetic words and many more, God birthed this ministry to help African-American and Hispanic people get into a position to lead. If you feel that the Lord is calling you to partner with us please let us know the part you should play in helping African-American and Hispanic people get in place. This ministry is not just for African-American people but it is for all cultures! **VOLUNTEERS ARE NEEDED!**

Chad Taylor
"Africa will become a Storehouse to the Nations--the Army and the Wealth of Esau is Coming Back"
Below is a prophecy Chad Taylor spoke over Africa, given on February 17, 2008 at Victory Christian Fellowship in Fresno, California:

Africa, mighty nation of kings and princes, the Lord says to

Africa, "Rachel, weep no more. Your children are coming back to their borders, and every anointing that was forfeited, sold and stolen, on every foreign seashore, will return to your continent a hundred fold in this lifetime and the life to come. For I see Esau coming back to Jacob; I see the army of Esau and all of his lambs and sheep. I see the wealth of Esau coming back to Jacob. I see the Queen of Sheba coming unto Solomon. I see the wealth of the wicked returning; returning to the shores of Africa. And you will rebuild the old waste places and the cities that have been ashes."

God will rise up before your eyes, even like a new Jerusalem, God will raise up a city, God will raise up a continent, and God will raise up a nation even in a day.

Esau, Jacob and the Spirit of Joseph

God says, "It will be a miracle; it will be a phenomena. It will be a paradox to some, a miracle to others, and a phenomena to not just a few with what I do through you, oh Africa. For the army and the wealth of Esau, and the birthright that was stolen and sold is coming back to Jacob."

I see ships, ships, ships full of your people, full of generations, full of mantles, full of anointing, and full of crowns coming back, filling your seashores and filling the horizons as far as the eye can see. From a thousand years ago until now, coming back, coming back, and coming back; for what the devil meant for evil, God has always intended for your good. And the spirit of Joseph shall rest upon you, and you will live in no pit and no prison any more. And the scepter of Pharaoh shall be extended to your nation and kings shall come to the brightness of its rising and the army of the gentiles shall come because the glory of the Lord is arising and shining upon you.

Storehouses to the Nations

God says, "And though gross darkness has covered you, My glory shall arise and shine upon you." For that very text of Scripture was written for such a time as this, and you will not fail in the time of testing and you will pour it back upon the King of kings and the Lord of lords. Great charity will break poverty, and Africa will become a storehouse to the nations. There will be storehouses filled with new manna and new bread, and other countries in the next decade will come to Africa to fill their bags and fill their ships. I will completely turn it around, for all things work together for the good of those called according to My purposes, and My purposes are coming into fullness, fullness, fullness.

And I am recapturing the minds of your youth. They will become doctors and they will become geniuses in their fields. They will become physicists and lawyers and they will defend you and they will stand for you. And I will raise them up to be the head and not the tail, as prophets and kings--as priests." Hallelujah! Hallelujah! Hallelujah! Hallelujah!

Signs and Wonders over Africa

It starts in 2008. The stall and the calves have left the gate in 2008, and you will see a phenomenon in the sky above; you watch it, you watch it. Those that are observant and those that are prophetic and even science shall record the mysteries and the signs and wonders in the heavens above and the earth beneath. Blood, fire and pillars of smoke shall be seen over Africa as a sign and a wonder and as a symbol of God's promises and His ability to perform them in this hour. Strange eclipses of the sun and the moon; strange phenomena in the heavens.

I hear the Lord saying, "A star is born, and kings will come to the brightness of its rising to bring their gifts, to bring their wealth and to bring their wisdom."

Hospitals, Universities and Technological Breakthroughs

I see medical hospitals and medical colleges rising up within Africa that will be the envy of the nations, and people will come there to attend those schools and those universities. Like Oxford was in England, God is raising up the academic anointing in the nation of Africa, and you will be the envy of England and the envy of America. Great medical institutions and great academic institutions shall rise from the ashes of civil war.

God says, "Where war has marked those countries, so shall My glory now mark them. I will remove the pricks that you have kicked against and I will remove the obstacles and I will make a way where there appeared to be in one day, no way."

Oh my God. Oh my God. And the Lord says, "I will break up the fountains of the deep and waters shall be found. Waters shall be discovered that will be bottled, that shall become an industrious witty-invention and will bring wealth to the people in Christian communities. Discoveries, hidden treasures in the darkness will be coming to the light, to the faithful few, and into the hands of the Joseph-anointed. For I am building an Ark in the continent of Africa, and many nations shall come to find the Glory that resides in you."

James W. Goll (Feb 4, 2011)
God and the Egyptian Crisis - a Redemptive Interpretation on the Descendents of Abraham

Abraham's wife Sarah lived almost 40 years after the birth of Isaac. Genesis 23:1–2 says: *"Now Sarah lived one hundred and twenty-seven years; these were the years of the life of Sarah. Sarah died in Kiriath-arba (that is, Hebron) in the land of Canaan; and Abraham went in to mourn for Sarah and to weep for her."*

Abraham loved Sarah dearly and must have experienced much grief and pain at her loss. After finding an excellent wife for his son Isaac, Abraham took another wife, whose name was Keturah. Genesis 25:2–4 says that Keturah bore to him Zimran and Jokshan and Medan and Midian and Ishback and Shuah. Jokshan became the father of Sheba and Dedan. And the sons of Dedan were Asshurim and Letushim and Leummim. The sons of Midian were Ephah and Epher and Hanoch and Abida and Eldaah. All these were the sons of Keturah. Keturah bore more children by Abraham than did Sarah and Hagar combined. I think that is interesting.

Before Abraham died he gave gifts to the sons of Keturah and sent them far away from his son Isaac, to the land of the east (see Genesis 25:6). One of the sons of Keturah was Midian, the father of the Midianites. Some of the descendants of Keturah went to what was called Persia. Others were, apparently, scattered into Assyria. Genesis 25:7–8 records: *"These are all the years of Abraham's life that he lived, one hundred and seventy-five years. Abraham breathed his last and died in a ripe old age, an old man and satisfied with life."* What a way to leave this Earth – as an old man satisfied with life, and with a lineage left behind!

Abraham's sons, Isaac and Ishmael, came together to bury their father in a cave. What a powerful statement! They came together – they united – to remember their father and put him to rest (see Genesis 25:9). I wonder if that could be a picture of things yet to come. Could it be that our Father will yet do such a work among the descendants of Abraham that they could come together in common purpose at some point and time in history?

Keturah's Descendants Will Praise the Lord

Isaiah prophesied about the descendants of Keturah, saying: *"A multitude of camels will cover you [Israel], the young camels of Midian and Ephah"* (Isaiah 60:6). Remember that Midian was a son of Keturah, and Ephah was her grandson. In the next part of this verse, Isaiah mentions yet another grandson of Keturah: Sheba. *"All those from Sheba will come; they will bring gold and frankincense, and will bear good news of the praises of the Lord."*

Where else have you heard of gold and frankincense together? They were two of the three gifts that the wise men brought to Jesus after His birth (see Matthew 2:1–12). I cannot confirm that the wise men were descendants of Keturah, but they did come from the east, where the descendants of Keturah had settled, and they certainly fit the description of Isaiah's prophecy. Whether this prophecy was fulfilled literally at the birth of the Messiah or is a prophecy for the future yet to come, the minimum we can agree on is that there is prophetic destiny upon the children of Keturah.

These people will rise up as people of wealth and will end up worshiping the one, true God. They will bring forth praise to the Lord!

Now let's go to the amazing prophecy of Isaiah, which has not yet been fulfilled. In this passage you will see the descendants of Hagar, Sarah and Keturah come together. As you read, keep in mind that Hagar was an Egyptian and that she returned to Egypt to find a wife for Ishmael, her half-Hebrew and half-Egyptian son. Remember, too, that the descendants of Keturah settled in Assyria and beyond. Isaiah 19:19-20, 23–25:

In that day there will be an altar to the Lord in the midst of the land of Egypt, and a pillar to the Lord near its border. It will become a sign and a witness to the Lord of hosts in the land of Egypt; for they will cry to the Lord because of oppressors, and He will send them a Savior and a Champion, and He will deliver them...

In that day there will be a highway from Egypt to Assyria, and the Assyrians will come into Egypt and the Egyptians into Assyria, and the Egyptians will worship with the Assyrians. In that day Israel will be the third party with Egypt and Assyria, a blessing in the midst of the earth, whom the Lord of hosts has blessed, saying, *"Blessed is Egypt My people, and Assyria the work of My hands, and Israel My inheritance."*

God is going to humble Egypt eventually, and Egypt is going to lift a cry for help. The Arabs are going to cry out due to the severity of their oppressors, and the Lord will manifest Himself as their Savior and Champion. After much pressure, and the probability of an all-out war in the Middle East, God will make Himself known to the Arabic peoples and they will turn to Him. Isaiah described the length to which they will go: *"They will even worship with sacrifice and offering, and will make a vow to the Lord and perform it"* (Isaiah 19:21). This not only means that they will have a God encounter, but that they will become true disciples and will walk in obedience.

Notice that this move of God will also impact Assyria: Turkey, Iraq, Iran and other Middle Eastern territories. Keturah's children were scattered throughout the vast lands of Assyria! They still have an identity today, but it is obscured because Abraham sent them all eastward into Trans Jordan and beyond (see Genesis 25:6).

Imagine – the very area of Asia Minor, where the early Church of Jesus Christ once flourished, and will rise again out of the ashes into genuine, vibrant worship. Lands that appear to be held captive to the devil through Islam will be delivered and cleansed of their impurity. After thousands of years of broken promises, hatred and enmity between Arabs and Jews, this will truly be a glorious day! A day in history when the curse is reversed and the blessing of the Lord emerges.

What a day that will be! I can only imagine!

The Middle East is indeed a complex knot, but the Holy Spirit loves brooding over a mess of darkness. He is an expert at this task. Remember that the first mention of the Holy Spirit is that He hovered over the face of the deep. God loves bringing order out of chaos. The Holy Spirit is a pro at creating change and making all things new!

There will be, according to Isaiah, a highway from Egypt to Assyria, and people will go freely back and forth – probably right through the middle of Israel – worshiping God together. I can only imagine!

All of Abraham's Seed Will Be Blessed

The end of Isaiah 19 is so powerful that I want you to read it again: Israel will be the third party with Egypt and Assyria, a blessing in the midst of the earth, whom the Lord of hosts has blessed, saying, *"Blessed is Egypt My people, and Assyria the work of My hands, and Israel My inheritance."* In Isaiah 19:24– it reads, *"Blessed are the descendants of Hagar, God's people! Blessed are the descendants of Keturah, the work of God's hands! Blessed are the descendants of Sarah, God's inheritance!"*

God is the supreme multitasker. He can accomplish more than one thing at a time! Biblical prophecy indicates that alongside God's gathering of the outcasts of Israel to their homeland, He is setting the stage to do a great work among all the descendants of Abraham. Surprise us all, O Lord. Let it be so!

Praying for All the Peoples of the Middle East

Isn't this good? God has declared a prophetic blessing over all the peoples of the Middle East, because they all have come from Abraham's seed. The devil has arisen; however, to thwart God's blessing. A holy war – an unholy war, rather – has raged for thousands of years. The conflict continues to intensify and a massive, satanic battle is coming. But I am here to declare that the Lord is going to pierce the veil of Islam. A move of God is going to come from out of Persia, out of Iraq, out of Syria, out of Lebanon, out of Egypt and, of course, out of Israel.

Times of Darkness Precede Times of Great Light

Now just to set the record straight: From the angle that I presently read the Scriptures, I see a lot of intense bickering and warfare yet to occur before the fullness of Isaiah 19 comes to pass. I am not an ostrich with my head buried in the sand! Isaiah 60:1–3 lays out a Scriptural principle that says a time of great darkness will precede the unveiling of a great light. Gentiles will come to the brightness of its shining, and even kings will bow to the brilliance of this great light. But first comes gross darkness. Consider with me now Psalm 83:3–8, 16–18: *"They make shrewd plans against Your people, and conspire together against Your treasured ones. They have said, "Come and let us wipe them out as a nation, that the name of Israel be remembered no more." For they have conspired together with one mind; against You they make a covenant: The tents of Edom and the Ishmaelites, Moab and the Hagrites; Gebal and Ammon and Amalek, Philistia with the inhabitants of Tyre; Assyria also has joined with them; they have become a help to the children of Lot...*

Fill their faces with dishonor, that they may seek Your name, O Lord. Let them be ashamed and dismayed forever, and let them be humiliated and perish, that they may know that You alone, whose name is the Lord, are the Most High over all the earth.

Many Bible teachers agree that this text has not yet been fulfilled. This particular group has not yet been brought into an alignment with this degree of hatred. The passage does not say "the peoples of the land of the north," nor does it say "Germany." In fact, even Egypt seems to be missing from this list! Who and what is this alliance that conspires together?

Psalm 83 describes vividly a troubling alignment set against a wearied Jewish state. Let's turn to the pen of Sandra Teplinsky for more details: "Verses 5–8 tell how every nation in the neighborhood (except Egypt) unites against Israel: Edom and the Ishmaelites (southern Jordan and Saudi Arabia); Moab (central Jordan) and the Hagrites (Syria and Arabia); Gebal (southern Jordan); Ammon (central Jordan) and Amalek (Sinai desert); Philistia (Gaza Strip area); Tyre (southern Lebanon) and Assyria (Syria/Iraq). Verse 4 sounds their bellicose battle cry: *"Come... let us destroy them as a nation, that the name of Israel be remembered no more."*

In some ways this is nothing new. As I laid out earlier the enemy has, from the inception of Israel's rebirth, been standing close by with a knife to cut her throat! How did God's prophetic psalmist respond to this threat? How should we respond when we see these things taking place? The psalmist calls for God to glorify Himself – to make His great name and His name alone known over all the Earth. God's goal in times of testing is to glorify Himself.

He will ultimately use the Arab/Palestinian-Israeli conflict to do it. He wants both blood-drenched peoples to know that He alone is most High – not Allah, not Judaism without Jesus, not global secular humanism, not anything. What if the eyes of the entire world were looking on at the moment of Israel's apparent, imminent destruction – the moment when God brings humiliation to the enemies of Israel for the purpose of releasing His grace upon them?

Light Will Overpower the Darkness

Darkness comes first, and then the light shines (see John 1:5). There has never been a contest between light and darkness. When you enter a house, you simply flip the switch and (if it is wired properly) the light always drives away the darkness. Darkness is a temporary state! I am here not to declare the revival of evil – there are plenty of top-selling authors who will do that for you. I am here to broaden our horizons and to help us peer into the redemptive purposes of God, even in the midst of the most stressful, difficult times of the ages. Light will overpower darkness; eventually, somehow – someday!

The Scriptures I have shared regarding God's promises to the descendants of Abraham are all for this purpose: to bring light and hope to the very dark situation in the Middle East. But if all we had was Joel's prophecy we would still be assured that, before this world comes to an end, God will pour out His Spirit on all people (see Joel 2:28–29).

Target Practice

Somehow we made it to our Target Practice and you are still with me! Whew! (I thought for a moment I might have lost you!) Now let's set our sights with more Scripture-based praying.

Scripture and Prayer from Isaiah 19:23–25: In that day there will be a highway from Egypt to Assyria, and the Assyrians will come into Egypt and the Egyptians into Assyria, and the Egyptians will worship with the Assyrians. In that day Israel will be the third party with Egypt and Assyria, a blessing in the midst of the earth, whom the Lord of hosts has blessed, saying, *"Blessed is Egypt My people, and Assyria the work of My hands, and Israel My inheritance."*

Heavenly Father, thank You for the many promises that You have given to me and that You will fulfill each one. Thank You that You will also fulfill every promise You made to Abraham and his descendants. Hasten the day when all the descendants of Abraham through Hagar, Sarah and Keturah will worship You together in one accord. I agree with Your Word that says the descendants of Keturah are the work of Your hands and will be a blessing in the Earth. I ask specifically that You would bless the descendants of Keturah and lead them to Yourself. Reveal to them that Yeshua is their Messiah. I ask that Jesus would receive the reward of His sufferings through these descendants of Abraham, for the glory of Your holy and righteous name. Amen.

Scripture and Prayer from Isaiah 60:6

The young camels of Midian and Ephah; all those from Sheba will come; they will bring gold and frankincense, and will bear good news of the praises of the Lord.

Father God, I ask that the "young camels" and all the descendants of Keturah would come to You and turn favorably toward Israel. Bless them. Multiply them. Prosper them. I ask that You would inspire them to use their wealth to bless Israel and the Kingdom of God. I ask that they would be known in the Middle East and in the Earth as bearers of the Good News of praises to the Lord. Establish them as worshipers of the God of their father, Abraham, for Your great name's sake. Amen.

Scripture and Prayer from Matthew 9:36–38

Seeing the people, He [Jesus] felt compassion for them, because they were distressed and dispirited like sheep without a shepherd. Then He said to His disciples, *"The harvest is plentiful, but the workers are few. Therefore beseech the Lord of the harvest to send out workers into His harvest."*

Father God, Your compassion burned in the heart of Your Son, Jesus. Turn the distress of Abraham's descendants into gladness and blessing. I ask that their souls would not be downcast, but that they would put their hope in the God of their father, Abraham. Transform their misguided ways and lead them in Your paths of righteousness. Cause them to hunger and thirst after righteousness. Send out workers into this harvest field to bring Your living waters to a dry and weary land. I ask that Your workers would reap a bountiful harvest for Your Kingdom's sake. Amen.

Scripture and Prayer from John 10:14–16

I am the Good Shepherd, and I know My own and My own know Me, even as the Father knows Me and I know the Father; and I lay down My life for the sheep. I have other sheep, which are not of this fold; I must bring them also, and they will hear My voice; and they will become one flock with one Shepherd.

Jesus, Yeshua, Messiah, You are a Good Shepherd and You know all Your sheep. You have laid Your life down for all the descendants of Abraham through Hagar, Sarah and Keturah.

Bring the descendants of Hagar and Keturah into Your fold. Quicken their ears to hear Your voice. I ask that they would join with the descendants of Israel so that all of Abraham's descendants will become one flock with You as their great Shepherd. You are a mighty God and You will bring Your word to pass for Your name's sake. Amen!

The Promised Son of Abraham

All three national families of Abraham have, by and large, failed to recognize the true Messiah, who is Yeshua, our Lord Jesus Christ. The Jews are still looking for their Messiah to appear, while the others do not even realize that they need one. Although most accept Mohammed and Jesus as prophets, they do not believe that a Messiah is necessary. Still the prophetic

Scriptures predict that these descendants of Abraham will accept the true Messiah at a critical point in time.

I love the language of Isaiah 19:20: *"He will send them a Savior and a Champion."* A champion shall come. A messenger of the new covenant will be sent to turn away ungodliness from Jacob. Yeshua, Jesus, the true Messiah, said it succinctly: *"I have other sheep, which are not of this fold; I must bring them also, and they will hear My voice; and they will become one flock with one Shepherd"* (John 10:16).

A great spiritual revival is on God's agenda, and it will encompass all the descendants of Abraham throughout the Middle East, from the Nile River to the Euphrates.

Note: With permission from James W. Goll, Praying for Israel's Destiny with Chosen Books.

Chapter Ten

My Commissioning

I feel like I needed to share with you what happened to me and the Spiritual Rights Movement in 2011.
I have been in conversation with Rabbi Curt Landry concerning a project that I want to do in Liberia, Africa called myrubbertree.com. This project is in relationship to African-American people helping rebuild the war torn nation of Liberia. There is a lot of history around Liberia in which it was a nation selected as an entry point for the Freed African Slaves to return to Africa once they were free.

I will give you more information about this at a later date. When the Freed African Slaves went to Liberia, they did the same thing to the Liberians that was done to them in America. They put the people in bondage, treated them poorly, took over their government, and introduced them to a mixed gospel with Jesus and the Masonic included.

Liberia is the second poorest nation in the world and the people are in desperate need of help. The Lord has shown me that another reason African-American people have been cursed is due to the injustices we did to Liberians. I have built a team of seven mountain people in Liberia on the ground as well as a team of seven mountain people here in the United States. I also plan to take a team to Liberia to speak to some of its government leaders about how we can help them rebuild. They have the first female president in Africa who is a non-corrupt leader.

Liberia used to be the second largest producer of rubber in

the world. Firestone Tire and Rubber Company has been there for more than 100 years oppressing the people and God wants to bring restoration to them. I want to start rubber tree farms, plant churches, schools, businesses, provide medical assistance and other help.

Since Rabbi Curt Landry has myolivetree.com, I asked for his help which he has kindly agreed. As he and I were talking he told me of his personal history with African-American people and how he has been looking for someone in the African-American culture to embrace and bring into the one new man. He also talked about the Prime Minister of Israel brother's blood being on the land in Uganda, Africa, which he has invited me to go with him and a team to speak to the current president and reconcile this matter. The Lord showed him that this is the key to freeing the entire continent of Africa and the African-American people.

I told him about the message that the Lord has given me in regards to the anti-Semitic spirit that is over the U.S. and other nations. He advised that I should come to the House of David and let him Commission me to take that word to this nation and to the nations on behalf of African-American and Jewish people. I took a Team of 11 African-American and Hispanic men and women to the House of David for my Commissioning on Friday, January 7, 2011 in order to reconnect to our Jewish heritage.

In the meantime, before going, the Lord downloads to me a message out of Genesis 25:1-6 about Abraham's second wife Keturah, a black woman, and how Abraham sent her sons away. While there:

1. We dealt with the story of Abraham and Keturah, his African wife, and their children.

2. We dealt with why Abraham gave all he had to Isaac because he was God's chosen from the wife of Sarah. We understood that God had chosen Isaac and that He is sovereign and can choose whoever He wants to choose.

3. We dealt with Abraham only giving Keturah's sons' gifts and sending them away.

What God revealed to me here is how those sons must have felt as their father sent them away. We found through study they were between the ages of 20-30 years possibly. (The ages where a lot of African-American and Hispanic men derail in life). We dealt with a list of emotions these young men could have experienced:

- Hurt and pain
- Orphan spirit
- Rejection
- Abandonment
- Anger
- Rebellion
- Stubbornness
- Hard heartiness
- Bitterness
- Jealousy and more

It also helped us understand that sometimes God allows things that we don't understand and those things sometimes cause pain. And that we have to understand again that Isaac was God's choice and that Abraham did what he thought was best and right by sending Keturah's sons away so that Isaac wouldn't have a problem with them later.

I preached this message at my church and such a deliverance swept the whole church. Men and women weeping and crying about the pain that Keturah's sons must have felt as they had to leave Abraham's house.

4. I lead us into some deliverance around the above spirits and then we went into some deep repentance:
- Forgave God for choosing Issac over us.
- Forgave Abraham for sending us away.
- Forgave Isaac for being chosen.
- Forgave Keturah for allowing this to happen to her sons.
- Forgave Isaac and Ismael for not including us in the burial of Abraham.

We repented for all the above feelings and asked God to forgive us for what we had done in the entire situation and going into idolatry. And even things that we did that we don't know about yet.

I feel like what is also happening by going to the House of David we are coming back into fellowship with our brother Isaac and our father Abraham and reconnecting with our Jewish Heritage. This will cause great healing and restoration to come to us and our people. It's almost like Esau and Jacob reuniting.

I'm sorry for this being so long but I like to keep my leaders informed about what I am doing and how God is moving in my life and what He has called me to do. I also solicit your prayers for all of these things.

The service: January 7, 2011 the First Sabbat/Sabbath of the Year. Rabbi spoke these things during the service:

Rabbi Landry began by decreeing that this Commissioning was most holy unto the Lord. He knew it was bigger than the House of David Ministries, Kingdom Culture Ministries, Inc., the Spiritual Rights Movement and all the things that we all do.

He told us that in 1994 he was attending Azusa Street Conference in Oklahoma City, Oklahoma and received a personal prophetic word. The word that there would be an army raised up in the African-American community that would stand with Israel, that there would be a Commissioning, that there would be a major healing that would take place.

I met Rabbi Landry around 2009 and when He heard me speak he said he knew I was to be the vessel that God would use. What a humbling moment and we give God all the glory for him choosing us in this hour. This Commissioning was going to bring healing not only to this nation but to the nations, to deliver us all from the orphan spirit and reconnect all of us to our father Abraham. He said there would be a time that we must all be holy unto the Lord, and that the Lord would do this work. Rabbi advised us that a seed about Africa was planted in the House of David, he has 26 sons in Uganda and God has uniquely connected them to Africa. And God has uniquely connected Africa to the House of David and it is time that we (Africa & African-Americans) come home! Until everybody returns home we lack the Father's will. There is no fullness of the Father until the children come home. He said tonight the Lord is bringing us home. God was commissioning all of us in the spirit.

Rabbi Landry also told us that there was a prophetic word spoken that there would be an apostolic work happening in the House of David. We were getting ready that night to operate in the protocol of the highest level of spiritual warfare. So that day Rabbi asked the Lord what is it that you would have us to do Lord?

The service started with the lighting of the Sabbath candles and we were to allow the oil to react to the heat. The light of revelation would come. Rabbi taught first on honor, by saying honor is a force just as faith is a force. It caused things to move in your life. Then he proceeded to release the blessing of honor and it was a verbal blessing to come to our hearts. He admonished us to leave all shame and insecurities that we all battle and all the doubts. He said I want you to leave them in the chair and imagine you have soul ties to them and they are all about one inch long and are as thin as a spider's web. Your soul needs to receive a fresh word. David prayed *"bless the Lord, oh my soul and all that is within me, bless His holy name."*

He said "This is a transformation of suddenly! This is a Moed (in Hebrew). Give an applause and not only welcome them into the House of David, but into the kingdom for what they have been called to do." He further said, "We have never understood true honor; I'm not talking about man worship. I'm talking about receiving the laborers that are here, in the priesthood. This is not the marketplace, this is to strengthen the priest with vision so the marketplace will follow. The marketplace hasn't followed because you have lacked honor. So, tonight we are putting it in order. Tonight is to honor the priest, that's why I have the rabbis watching, you have lacked honor, don't be ashamed of who you are. You can only be who you are. Honor rests on truth, honor does not rest on lies. You are the workmanship that Paul talks about in Ephesian and you were handpicked before for such a time as this.

Then he proceeded to honor each of us individually. We celebrate faces and we honor your faces and we honor what God is doing in our presence. You are in David's house and David welcomes you home that you might sit and eat at the king's table, like Mepheboseth all the days of his life and not be told anything different.

He said we decree and agree we welcome the Office of the Prophet in the House of David, we welcome the Office of Apostle in the House of David, it is biblical and upon this rock the Lord will build His church and the gates of hell will not prevail against it. This is what the Lord is going to do tonight. It's the word that will not come back void. It's the word that will accomplish what it is sent to do. It's the word that the angels harken to Psalm 103:20.

As I prayed today Dr. Battle, I asked the Lord what is it you want to do in this Commissioning. So this is the word, so we are going to lay the word down as the foundation in the atmosphere, everything in the earth, under the earth, and in the atmosphere will bend its knee to this word.

Because this is a sacred assembly, this is a Commissioning. When I get done with this then Dr. Bigpond is going to welcome this word into his land. This is going to flow; all my fountains are in you, oh Zion, we are reversing the flow, in this nation from coming from the United States to Israel.

The way it should have always been; this is why the transference of wealth is coming in 2011, because the flow of the Spirit through the priest, it is coming out of Mt. Zion into the gate (Dr. Bigpond) and out. And we are in full agreement. There are not any strangers on this platform. Pastor Osborne, who is also first nations, we have been together for 10 years. I want you to hear what the Lord says He is going to do tonight.

Isaiah 45:19-25 (NKJ)

Isaiah 45:19 – *"I have not spoken in secret, In a dark place*

*of the earth; I did not say to the seed of Jacob, 'Seek Me in vain';
I, the LORD, speak righteousness, I declare things that are right.*

Isaiah 45:20 - *"Assemble yourselves and come; Draw near
together, You [who have] escaped from the nations. They have no
knowledge, Who carry the wood of their carved image, And pray
to a god [that] cannot save.*

Isaiah 45:21 – *"Tell and bring forth [your case]; Yes, let them
take counsel together. Who has declared this from ancient time?
[Who] has told it from that time? [Have] not I, the LORD? And
[there is] no other God besides Me, A just God and a Savior;
[There is] none besides Me.*

Isaiah 45:22 – *""Look to Me, and be saved, All you ends of
the earth! For I [am] God, and [there is] no other.*

Isaiah 45:23 – *"I have sworn by Myself; The word has gone
out of My mouth [in] righteousness, And shall not return, That to
Me every knee shall bow, Every tongue shall take an oath.*

Isaiah 45:24 – *"He shall say, 'Surely in the LORD I have
righteousness and strength. To Him [men] shall come, And all
shall be ashamed Who are incensed against Him.*

Isaiah 45:25 – *"In the LORD all the descendants of Israel
Shall be justified, and shall glory.' "*

He said this is that which Apostle Paul spoke of when he said be
not ignorant of this mystery and that you become bold in your own
opinion. That blind in part happened to the Jews so that the Gentiles
might be grafted in. For Abraham sinned when he lied in Egypt.

God may have chosen Isaac, but He has blessed Keturah's
seed. He has blessed Ishmael's seed. He has blessed all. He
gave His only begotten Son Yeshua, His blood removed the
wall of separation created in Himself one man from the two.
That which you see today and that which you stand today and

that which you are watching today, this is that that Apostle Paul spoke of.

How good and how pleasant for brethren to dwell together in unity! It is like the precious ointment that runs down the head, beard, and garment of Aaron, It is like the dew of Hermon and it is there where God himself commands the blessings of life forever.

The wisdom of Solomon; the wisdom that our brother Solomon had will be released tonight (he started to lay hands on us). For you are called like Esther, He called you for such a time as this, He has brought you out of all places, out of the House of David to flow, a flow **of reconciliation and stirring** up of the gifts of God. This is what the Lord says He shall do. Lord, we receive this word from the prophet Isaiah, we receive this word from King David, we receive this word from his son Solomon as an inspired word of the living God that shall not come back void but shall prosper in that which it is sent to do. We receive it in our life tonight and Lord we know that it shall and will prosper and change the atmosphere and change the universe. Father in the name of Yeshua we welcome and give this promise to the United States of America as a goodwill Ambassador from the nation of Israel, as an apostolic leader from Israel. We release this to our first nation's apostolic brother Lord. We ask that you will receive this gift as one, as the Lord has made us one. We walk in one accord – the tri-unity of peace. Lord, we ask now for on our land, these United States of America, that this word would flow in and transform and reconcile, and destroy all the works of the enemy. Let it be done tonight, all the works of the enemy plan to do between us in war be stopped in one night, in Jesus name.

Then Dr. Bigpond ministered, "he said honor and beauty should be released where we go. All the lands you go to release it. Always carry honor and beauty, carry it well and release it to my sons and daughters." He then came down and laid hands on each of us and released beauty and honor.

There is much more that goes in here!!!!!

Rabbi Landry and Dr. Bigpond went to Mt. Zion where God made a covenant with Abraham and they restored covenant with Abraham. Then they went to Mt. Hebron and picked up the Mantle of King David. They moved it from Hebron to Zion, from Zion to the House of David and from here to Dr. Battle. If you will receive it, this will change your life. You will say less and get more done.

Then Dr. Bigpond ministered, and said, "Honor and beauty should be released wherever we go. All the lands you go to, release it. Always carry honor and beauty, carry it well and release it to my sons and daughters."

Wow! I've been shot out of a cannon. Praise the Lord! We did make it back into Georgia before the storm. Below are a couple of pictures from the Commissioning as well as it was shown live on streaming television. To God be all the glory, all the honor, and all of the praise for what He is doing in all of our lives!

Rabbi Curt Landry & his wife, Apostle Nigel Bigpond, and pastor, on January 7, 2011.
Dr .Venessa Battle at the Commissioning on January 1, 2011.

There were many more prophetic words and signs and wonders that took place. The bottom line was God was restoring Keturah and her sons back to Isaac and Abraham.

May 3, 2011 I went to Memphis, Mississippi, and Marion, Arkansas

Rabbi Landry was preaching and there was an amazing time in the earth. The anointing was extremely strong. A word of wisdom and knowledge came from Rabbi Landry that stated that this area of the country was a seat of government and out of that area (we are sure that we were not the only people praying) but America's number one arch enemy (Osama Bin Laden) was captured that night. Also, a word came forth by the spirit of God through me that the gas prices must go down now in Jesus' name. That Monday in the *Reuters* it was reported that gas prices had plunged for no apparent reason. What had happened? Well what we believe is that in Alabama the sons of Abraham had gathered together. We had someone represent Isaac, Ishmael, Keturah's sons, the Native Americans and the church had gathered in unity. When the church comes to this type of unity and all the sons of Abraham are gathered, we will become unstoppable!

Chapter Eleven

"Breaking Curses"

African-American curses can be traced from Africa to America to the present day. Blacks betrayed blacks by capturing and selling them for slaves in other lands. Then came slavery to America. Out of slavery came curses on blacks and on America. Slavery created practices that continue today. (See Appendix 3, Curses) Witchcraft was practiced in Africa, and the slaves brought witchcraft to America. From slavery came witchcraft curses on blacks and America. The practice of witchcraft continues today. The judgment of GOD is on Americans for slavery, witchcraft and other sins.

Slavery

Katrina, the name of the hurricane that hit New Orleans in 2005, is the goddess of witchcraft, tombs, demons and the underworld (vampires, spirits, werewolves, etc.). David Dreiling said that GOD revealed to him that the hurricanes had to do with slavery. That is why they formed mysteriously off the coast of West Africa. Hurricanes, in hurricane alley, follow the slave trade routes to the Americas.

African-American Experience
(Ministering Deliverance Within The Context of The African-American Experience)

These are some comments for African-American people:

1. They hold onto secrets and the dark side of life. They are tied-up in emotions. **They need to put their emotions on the table and deal with the issues, hurts, fears and anger.**

2. They seek approval, but reject it out of fear of the wrong motives of others. The way they treat each other is the way they treat God. When they are overloaded, they cannot stay connected to God. They pull back from God and walk away.

3. The Church is not healthy and not dealing with its own issues. The inward child spirit (boy/girl) gets in the way. Fear is tied to childhood. They are kicking at the pricks.

4. There has been a raw hatred of the race in America. They have become prejudiced and bitter. Those who are older have seen the physical or emotional lynching of people and careers. They hate self because of color. There is a light/dark skin issue. The ceiling to God has become brass and the Earth has become iron. Sometimes when they are side-by-side with a white person, the white person is favored in housing, check-out counter, etc.

5. They hate themselves, but won't admit it. They will change their face and hair to appear whiter. They feel racist but must deal with it as a Christian. **Slavery has brought a curse on them.** They were beaten into submission. It was planned, perpetuated and thought biblical by whites. **The curse must be broken so that the Earth yields its fruits, and they have favor with God and man.**

6. Preachers dispel the myth as head over the body as being prosperous and well thought. People take care of expenses of family, come to him, drive a nice car, and still have spirits over them. They have bought a car and several suits with Anniversary Week for the pastors. They may have more than

one wife and several families even in the same church; one would be legal with the other common law.

7. In slavery, black preachers were given free rein on the plantation with the women who were encouraged to believe in God. He could go from house to house, which was expected. He was fed and lay with the women. **These spiritual curses must be broken.**

8. They could be sold to another plantation and start a new family. Children were considered promise seeds to work on the plantation. Black males still do that today and may have many children. This is African culture when man is not the husband of one wife.

9. The Devil needs to be exposed. It doesn't have to be like this. People are blind to the light of God. They must learn what the Scriptures say about them. This is a carryover from slavery and is passed down through generations.

10. Churches need to change and take the lead with a strong voice. There needs to be teaching of the truth where God will be allowed to act. God's anointing will flow with the answers. **Chains and bondage can be broken.**

11. We can set-up an operating room and recovery room for deliverance patients. **They have to break the demonic patterns handed down through the generations.** They may need to be filled with The Holy Spirit.

12. No father at home brings rejection. They need the love of The Father God to be approved and accepted.

13. The altar should be open during the service and The Holy Spirit allowed freedom to act. **Imputation and anointing of The Father's love needs to be ministered.**

Breaking The Curse Off Black America

The African-American race labors under tremendous curses and afflictions. Many were high on crack cocaine, drunk on alcohol, unwed teenage mothers walking around with babies in their arms, young people driving expensive cars obtained largely from drug sale profits, ladies purposely dressed seductively, and young men exposing their underwear. Further, a staggering number of African-American males are filling the prisons, embracing homosexuality, prostitution and all sorts of perversion.

The result of disobedience is death. God's reward for sin, iniquities, perversions, and those who walk contrary to His Word is death - natural and spiritual.

There are various types of perversions: spiritual, sexual, financial, and others. Financial perversion encompasses - but is not limited to - cheating, stealing, robbery, bribes, covetousness, deceit, gambling, and unlawful gain. Perverse speech denotes lying, slander, cursing and swearing, and speaking blasphemous words.

African-Americans are a people born of the seed of slavery. The mixture of races of Africans, Europeans, and Indians has produced a mixed breed now called African-American. Black America is under a curse of plagues and vexations resulting in calamities - instead of blessings - overtaking them. Blessings and curses rest upon families, communities, and even entire nations.

An apparent consequence of the history of enslavement, bondage, and oppression is two-fold: the belief of many Black Americans that they will never be free; and the opportunity that this belief provides for Satan to establish stronghold over this people.

Among legally married persons, regardless of geographic region in the U.S., blacks are at greatest risk. Young black males are dying untimely deaths - it's a war zone of mass destruction. It is a perpetuated cycle of poverty and crime in the black community.

Forty million babies have been killed by abortion since 1973 when abortion was legalized, and 14 million of them were black. The aim of the program was to restrict – and many believe, exterminate - the black population with the Negro Project.

Black leaders must teach the truth from their pulpits, live the truth daily, and avoid making excuses for their insufficiencies. Therefore, some of the conditions under which many of the people exist are the primary responsibility of black church leaders.

The prevalence of high blood pressure in blacks in the United States is among the highest in the world. Blacks have almost twice the risk of first-ever strokes compared with whites. Among the leading cancers, prostate cancer among black men is about 15 times higher than among white men and 2.7 times higher than among Asian/Pacific Islander men.

In studies that compare individuals with similar levels of income and education, blacks have a shorter life expectancy than any other racial group. The Census Bureau indicated that by 2010 there would be only 85 black men for every 100 black women.

The lack of parental involvement has caused low self-esteem, lack of motivation to learn, laziness, apathy, and a lack of accountability among too many young people. Many are growing up uncovered, unprotected, unnourished, without a father, abandoned, rejected, and dealing with generational curses and emptiness left by the absence of a father.

Approximately 25 per 1,000 black children were confirmed victims of maltreatment, more than double the national average and the highest victimization rate among racial groups represented.

HIV was the number one cause of death for blacks between the ages of 25 and 44 in 2000. In 2002, the leading cause of HIV infection among black men was sexual contact with other men (sodomy or homosexual activity) followed by injection drug use and heterosexual contact. In 2002, blacks had the highest STD rates in the nation. Of new infections among men in the United States, approximately 60% were infected through homosexual sex, 25% through injection drug use, and 15% through heterosexual sex.

If the sin was sexual, it could bring adultery, incest, children from incestuous union, children born out-of-wedlock, destroy virginity, bestiality, homosexuality, lesbianism, and sodomy. Other curses come from parents, pastors, rulers, and authorities turning away from God, idolatry, pride, fleshly practices, and touching or harming God's anointed.

There are very few members living according to biblical principles, including the pastor and deacons. In reality, man-made traditions, man-made customs, and simply put, the flesh, are the guiding factors of the church. Sin is rampant with God appearing to be powerless to stop it. There is a lack of integrity of the ministerial leadership, negative strongholds, bondages, and traditions within the Black Church. The profaneness has been released upon Black America by spiritual leaders. Black America has paid a dear price for ignorance. The immoral activities and sensual behavior patterns have cost families and, in some case, lives.

The Civil Rights era was a turning point for Black America. After many protests, beatings, persecution, and marches, blacks began to be recognized as a people. The Rev. King's sexual escapades were intertwined with his manhood just like other men of the cloth who were preoccupied or infatuated with love. We can determine that after the Rev. Dr. Martin L. King, Jr. died, the symptoms of the curse broke forth and continued to multiply even until today. The Southern Christian Leadership Conference (SCLC) was a rowdy group engaged in partying, prostitution and even sexual harassment. There was a great release of spiritual profaneness by black leaders that has continued to this day.

If church leaders are living in sin, what can be expected from Black America? There is no need to cover-up and shift the blame to others and continue to play the victim.

Christians are just churching, and sin is running rampant in the church, especially among today's leaders. It's the 'don't do as I do, do as I say' principle. For years, deceit, mistrust, and lack of spiritual discipline and truth have eroded these once hallowed organizations.

Today, more than ever before, men of the cloth are fornicating and having children by women within their congregations. Sexual immoralities and perversion abide more inside the church than outside the church. All they can see is fame and fortune, but few look deep into the hurts, fears, and weaknesses of those who give the appearance that all is well.

We are beholding the fruit of sin, and it seems that whatever we wanted to happen is operating in reverse. Judges have been led away in handcuffs, and some black judges have been disbarred. A dark cloud appears to hover over Black America and the people are engulfed in a culture of sin. The Democratic Party is consistently on the wrong side of moral issues leading the way for abortion and homosexuality legislation. A culture of sin has fallen upon the black community, and it is in denial and refuses to hear the truth. Immorality is running rampant, touching every sector of the black community, starting with the leaders.

Many churches are in need of help, not having good leadership. There are pastors who cannot be found. There are ladies in churches who are laboring, even when men cannot be found and leadership is lacking.

Be assured, no matter how small the sin, it will be exposed when God reveals it in His own time. Many pastors and leaders are fully aware of the sins and demonic strongholds with which they are living. Many pastors are living a lie. Their main concern is for wealth and status.

Spiritual darkness is encountered everywhere. Some well-known preachers are living a lie. Many leaders in the Black Church are stumbling repeatedly as though the Lord cannot direct their path. There are bad batches of worship and praises going up to God in the black churches.

Much of the work of the Black Church is acceptable to man, but not unto God as it is done grudgingly and of necessity. There is a dire need for black leaders to see clearly in the Spirit. There is too much immorality in the Black Church, namely greed, pedophilia, homosexuality, lesbianism, adultery, and fornication. Immorality, unethical practices, and evil have spread in the church.

Homosexuals are directing church choirs and many homosexuals are taking over the music ministries (pastors are being held hostage). Some are pastors and members of the clergy. The poverty and slavery mentality needs to be transformed, and strongholds of hopelessness and despair destroyed. Self-hatred and hatred for others needs to diminish. Black America needs to humble itself, and confess and repent for its sins and shortcomings on a national basis.

Sexually wounded and scarred females and males need to be healed. They have been victims to mental and physical illnesses, witness protection programs, drug rehabilitation centers, and welfare institutions. If God's call is not heeded and His cure not responded to, the curses will worsen.

Races And Cultures

The names for races and cultures have changed through the years. Negro has become **Black, Black American**, Afro-American and African-American, the latter the present preferred designation. Spanish has become Latin-Oriented, **Latin American and Hispanic**. This is a short version of the experience as written by Vunetia Mosley of the Fresh Anointing International Church in Birmingham, Alabama.

Breaking The Willie Lynch Curse

This is American slavery; slavery in the West Indies is similar. I am going to read **"Breaking the Willie Lynch Curse,"** which was provided by Stan and Elizabeth of demonbuster.com. This is very powerful and apparently was inspired by Satan and his demons. **You can see these characteristics in the Black race of people.** This could be the very reason why so many are on welfare today. The curse must be broken off your blood line. Can you recognize these characteristics in your race?

Effects

Today with the use of drugs, fear, distrust, envy and murders, we can see the effects of these terrible curses. The Lord gave the revelation of the Willie Lynch curse to a friend of ours. After breaking this curse, she felt a release. Others have commented that they too have felt a release from this curse.

Let's Make A Slave - The Origin and Development of a Social Being Called The Negro. Many people argue about whether or not this is true. If you look at what a slave was reduced to I would agree that somebody somewhere had an evil Satan backing plan to destroy the African people. This book written by William Lynch outlined the methods that he used to control the slaves he owned. These methods placed many curses on the black race, even keeping them in bondage today. He also told the people to have their white servants and their overseers to distrust all blacks.

Quote by Willie Lynch

In my bag here, I have a foolproof method for controlling your black slaves. I guarantee every one of you that, if installed correctly, it will control the salves for at least 300 years.

Speech

William Lynch was a white slave owner, who reportedly made a speech on the banks of the James River in 1712. In this speech, Lynch spoke of having methods to control slaves. These methods could have only come from Satan himself. Lynch used fear, distrust, envy and beatings. He even went as far as murdering the males in front of the women and children in order to control the minds of the slaves.

He went on to say that the slave, after receiving this indoctrination, would carry on the practice. It would become self-refueling and self-generating for hundreds of years, maybe even thousands. He told them that by killing the protective male image, it would throw the females into a frozen psychological state of independency. This would result in her raising her offspring into reverse positions.

The female offspring would be taught to be like herself, independent and negotiable. The male offspring would be raised to be mentally dependent and weak. He said that the owners were to cause the young men, old men and the females to distrust each other. However, make the slaves trust and depend on the owners and their families.

Lynching

It has been said that the term lynching came from this man. He apparently would lynch slaves as a means to control other slaves. There is still some vigilante action in the world today taken primarily against the Black race by the White race. There is a fear of Black race being lynched by White people.

The term lynching can also be applied without hanging. It can be used for unjust treatment of the Black race in their personal lives, their ministry lives and in their business lives. They are essentially "lynched" out of what is rightfully theirs.

Our Ministry

"Our ministry started in the African-American churches. We minister to African-Americans in church and in our home. God gave us a burden to help set my brothers and sisters free. This is a partial lesson about how to minister to the Black race that has bondage that originates in Africa." - Apostle Gene Moody

Prayer

Lord Jesus Christ, I forgive Willie Lynch and all those involved in slave trade and slave use throughout time whether in the black or white race. I forgive those who treat the black race as slaves today. I forgive all who want to lynch me personally, ministerially and business-wise today. I pray that you would forgive and bless them with spiritual blessings, especially salvation.

In the Name of Jesus Christ, I break the curse of Willie Lynch off of me and my bloodline going back to 1712 and earlier. I now break all curses placed on me by those involved in slavery and those who treat me like a slave. I command the demons restore to me and my family everything that they have stolen from us. I command this in the name of Jesus Christ, my Savior, Lord and Master. Amen.

Deliverance

I now command every demon whose legal right has been taken away by this prayer to manifest and leave me. I command the spirits of drug addiction, fear, distrust, envy, murder, control, physical abuse, frozen psychic, demonic independence, mental weakness, lynching spirit, vigilante spirit and related spirits to go. I do this by the power and blood of Jesus Christ, and the authority invested in me by being a Christian. Amen.

Breaking Strongholds In The African- American Family

These are characteristics of African-Americans. Do you recognize these characteristics?

Relationships

Black Men: You can't trust black women in some cases. Black women are mean, spiteful, and they use you. Women are only good for having babies and cooking. You have to slap a woman around every now and then. You have to love them and leave them.

Black Women: All black men are dogs. Women must take charge and never let a man control them. I can't live without this man. He beats me, but he's a good man.

Black Youth: My parents don't deserve obedience.

Morality and Character

Black Men: It's all right to have more than one woman. Drugs and alcohol are not that bad. The only thing that is important is what you do for yourself.

Black Women: You've got to sleep with a man in order to get him.

Black Youth: Everybody else is doing it and so can I. I will do whatever I want. I will hurt others before I hurt myself. I have to do whatever to look cool to my friends and I have to have sex to be accepted by my homeys.

Religion

Black Men: I am God, in some cases, not all. The Bible is the white man's religion. Islam is the black man's religion and the Masons are a good thing.

Black Women: Following my horoscope is all right to engage in and to use to find a mate. Eastern Star is a good thing. Islam is the black man's religion. The church is full of hypocrites. Christianity is a crutch for weak black folks. The Masons are a good thing. I go to church, but I need some stuff from the occult shop, too.

Black Youth: There is no God, in some cases, not at all.

Prayer

I forgive all black men, black women and black youth for the way they have treated me. Forgive me for the way I have treated them. In Jesus Name I pray. Amen.

Deliverance

I command the spirits of distrust, meanness, spitefulness, physical abuse, unfaithfulness, control, disobedience, adultery, fornication, drug addiction, alcoholism, murder, hate, horoscopes, Eastern Star, Islam, hypocrisy, and Masonry to manifest and leave me in the Name of Jesus Christ.

143

Religious Spirits

Control Spirits

Control By The Church, Control Spirits Of The Bishop Or Preacher, Spirits In Preachers Using Voodoo In Their Ministry To Control People, Loosing Those Who You Worked Voodoo On In The Past, or Evil Soul Ties With The Bishop Or Preacher.

False Spirits

False Praise, False Worship, False Holy Dance, False Shouting Spirits, False Dancing In The Spirit, False Voodoo Tongues, False Prophecy, False Baptism Of Fire, False Visions And Dreams, False Voices Calling Themselves God, or False Preaching Spirits.

Witchcraft and Voodoo Spirits

Voodoo Spirits, Voodoo Dancing, Jerking Spirits, Shaking Spirits, Quivering Spirits, Spirits That Cause The Body To Twitch, Rocking Backward And Forward Spirits During Preaching And Worship, Spirits That Make The Eyes Roll Back In The Head During Praise, Burning In The Stomach Called The Holy Ghost, Fire Walking Spirits, Veil Over The Eyes Spirit, or Spirits Of Divination

List Of Demon
(Ministering Deliverance Within The Context Of The African-American Experience)

Prayers
Sins / Curses / Demons
Deuteronomy 27 and 28 Leviticus 26:40

Various Demons evil soul ties, sins of ancestors; false self-respect, power, dignity and confidence; word curses, desire for ungodly power and control, lack of family commitment or commitment to relationships, failure to thrive, forced submissiveness, loss of sons, blind justice, unworthiness, son of Belial, lack of peace, drive by killings, prison bars, slave labor, prejudice, racism, divorce, misplaced and misguided desires, drug sales, poor responsibility and accountability, emotional hurricane, deep sorrow, souls for sale, false prosperity, lack of trust, betrayal, invisibility, pretty children, gold dust, tradition, gambling spirit, divorce, broken marriages, families in rebellion, intimidation, unsaved children and teenagers, loneliness, rejection from the main stream culture, rejection from our spouses, wicked thoughts, stealing other's reputations, coveting, slander, gossip, maliciousness, unholy affections. hurt, sorrow, racist, ungodliness, oppression, temper outburst, refusal behaviors, disgust, failure, beating, lynching, abandonment, loneliness, self-destruction, multiple personalities, double mindedness, schizophrenia, disassociation, pride (Leviathan, strength in his neck), lack of ability to give or receive love, animal spirits, aggression, hollowness, hunger, abduction, kidnap, unbelief, unproductiveness, rage, self-serving spirits, deception, ugly spirit, arrogance, vain imaginations, fits of rage, acrimony, unpleasantness, sullenness, animosity, hostility, provocation, vexation, grief, sorrow, upheaval, insurgence, mutiny, revolution, contentiousness, disputing, stubborn-headed, rebellious attitude against God, defiance, accepts no correction, provoking rejection, stiff-nakedness, overthrowing, destructive, convulsive, resistive, interfering, friction withstanding, repulsiveness, aggression, daring, scornfulness, confusion, division, ridicule, tension, hurt, insults, frustration, disgust, insecurity, difficulty learning, discord, selfishness, doubt, inability to achieve, fake sickness, hypochondriacs, and domination.

Sex

Rape, birthing illegitimate children, teen pregnancy, prostitution, men sharing, women sharing, low morals, lust not love, barrenness, bastard, flirting, sexual sin, abortions, sexual abuse of children, perversion, homosexuality, seduction, fornication, abuse and rape of women, power in the penis (Behemoth, strength in his loins), sexual promiscuity, adultery, fornication, incest, lust, sodomy, pornography, lesbianism, sex toys, oral sex, anal sex, and bestiality.

Infirmity

Infirmity, high blood pressure, heart disease, arthritis, lupus, cancer, stroke, hardening of arteries, mental illness, worry, pandemonium, anxiety, and pharmacies.

Death

Death, destruction, Abaddon, Apollyon, suicide, abortion, murder and other crimes, death sentence, and early death.

Religion

False doctrine, abuse of Scripture; false prophesy, wealth or prosperity; spiritual status, false prestige, preacher's whoop/squall, smooth talking, power of persuasion, domination, manipulation and control, straddling the fence, charmer, spiritual ambitious, lack of accountability, compromise, cover-up, attitude of superiority, verbal and physical abuse, spiritual weakness, vain arguments, profane fictions, abuse of titles, silly myths, irreverent babble, godless chatter, demonic intercessory prayers, Rastafarianism, village shrine rituals, worship and open relationship with the dead, Orisa Worship (Yoruba), Voodoo (Vodun), ancestor reverence and worship, Religion (magic and healing), spiritualism, witchcraft, nature worship, incense burning, psychic prayers, spirit possession, abuse by men of the cloth, idolatry, Islam, and church splits.

Addictions

Addictions (drugs, cigarettes, alcohol, prescription drugs, gambling, excessive spending), self-destruction through use of substances to hide pain, and obesity (overweight, love for food, gluttony, overeating, I'm Fat spirit).

Slavery

Slavery, spirits of fear, distrust, envy, murder, control, physical abuse, frozen psychic, demonic independence, mental weakness, lynching spirit, vigilante spirit, and related spirits.

Black Interaction

Spirits of distrust, meanness, spitefulness, physical abuse, unfaithfulness, control, disobedience, adultery, fornication, drug addiction, alcoholism, murder, hate, horoscopes, Eastern Star, Islam, hypocrisy, and Masonry.

Occult

Roots, Dr. Buzzard, oils (potions, powders, incense), dream books, numerology and other forms of divination, black, white and candle magic, dreams, incantation, superstition, occult, Herbal Medicine, divination, sorcery, medium ship, necromancy, kinship and royal rituals, ancestral intervention, and reincarnation.

Black

Down playing or hatred of African features (hair, nose, mouth, skin color), black hatred, hatred for whites, darkie, blackie, black pride, African pride, unlawful transfer of property belonging to blacks, lack of inheritance, and poverty.

Demonic Tongues

Tongue of strange woman and of the serpent, vipers, flattering, smooth, slandering, deceitful, sharp, proud, lying, false, backbiting, stammering, crafty, confused, striving, devises mischief, full of adder's poison, forward, naughty, perverse, evil fire, double, full of trouble, sin, mischief and iniquity.

Matriarchal

Matriarchal hierarchy due to absence of men in spirit and/

or body, matriarchal headed homes, absent fathers, improper family structure, improper male/female relationships, improper alignment, Jezebel and Ahab spirits

Pray deliverance prayers for anger we must:

- Forgive God for choosing Isaac over us.
- Forgive Abraham for sending us away
- Forgive Isaac for being chosen
- Forgive Keturah for allowing this to happen to her sons.
- Forgive Isaac and Ishmael for not including us in burial of Abraham.

We need to repent for all the above feelings and ask God to forgive us for what we have done in this entire situation and going into idolatry. And even things that we did that we don't yet know about.

Chapter Twelve

The Ministry of Reconciliation

The Bible has a lot to say about reconciliation and it is a very important concept to the gospel of Jesus Christ. The enemy has done and is trying to do everything he can to keep the body of Christ separated and at odds. Paul says in 2 Corinthians 5:17-21:

17) "Therefore, if anyone is in Christ, he is a new creation; old things have passed away; behold, all things have become new.

18) "Now all things are of God, who has reconciled us to Himself through Jesus Christ, and has given us the ministry of reconciliation,

19) "That is, that God was in Christ reconciling the world to Himself, not imputing their trespasses to them, and has committed to us the word of reconciliation.

20) "Now then, we are ambassadors for Christ, as though God were pleading through us: we implore you on Christ's behalf, be reconciled to God.

21) "For He made Him who knew no sin to be sin for us, that we might become the righteousness of God in Him."

Reconcile defined - the Greek word for reconcile is katallasso which means exchange, to change mutually, to change from enmity to friendship. (*Strongs*)

According to Webster, it means "to cause (a person) to accept or be resigned to something not desired; to cause to become friendly again, to compose or settle (a quarrel, dispute); to bring into agreement or harmony, to restore.

It means to change from ill will or hostility against man to friendship. Paul talks about reconciliation between God and man. There is/was enmity between God and man because of man's sin. Enmity between God and man has nothing to do with something being wrong with God but it has to do with man operating in a life of sin. Isaiah 59:1-2 says it like this:

1) *"Behold, the LORD's hand is not shortened, That it cannot save; Nor His ear heavy, that it cannot hear.*

2) *"But your iniquities have separated you from your God; and your sins have hidden His face from you, so that He will not hear."*

Thank God that the gospel proclaims how God has a desire to reconcile man back to Himself. We must understand that when people need to reconcile to each other, it is normally because the fault lies on both sides. This is not the case between man and God. It is man who is at fault because man has usually moved away from God; therefore, man needs to be reconciled back to God, not God back to man.

Reconciliation is made possible to man because of what Jesus Christ did on the cross by dying or mankind's sin. Colossians 1:19-21 says for it pleased the Father that in Him all the fullness should dwell, and by Him to reconcile all things to Himself, by Him, whether things on Earth or things in Heaven, having made peace through the blood of His cross. And you, who once were alienated and enemies in your mind by wicked works, yet now He has reconciled.

It is only through Jesus Christ that man can be reconciled to God. God used Christ who did not know sin to represent our sin and be punished by His death for our sins. We were enemies and alienated from God because of that sin in our lives. But God, provided us a way back to Him and way for us to be reconciled to Him through His only begotten Son Jesus Christ. God loves us so much that he provided us a way back to Him. John 3:16 says, *"For God so loved the world that He gave His only begotten Son, that whoever believes in Him should not perish but have everlasting life."* Through Christ's death we became the righteousness of God in Him. According to Colossians 1:21-22, *"And you, who once were alienated and enemies in your mind by wicked works, yet now He has reconciled, in the body of His flesh through death, to present you holy, and blameless, and above reproach in His sight."*

And Romans 4:4-8 says, *"Now to him who works, the wages are not counted as grace but as debt. But to him who does not work but believes on Him who justifies the ungodly, his faith is accounted for righteousness, just as David also describes the blessedness of the man to whom God imputes righteousness apart from works: "Blessed are those whose lawless deeds are forgiven, And whose sins are covered; Blessed is the man to whom the LORD shall not impute sin."*

We also can be holy, blameless and above reproach because Jesus became propitiation for our sin! Propitiation means to make favorable or to appease. Appease means "to satisfy, relieve, to yield to the demands of" (*Webster*). There was a price that had to be paid for man's sins, Jesus Christ was used to satisfy the demands of God to have a sinless perfect one to pay the price. Here are some other Scriptures that speak about reconciliation:

Daniel 9:24 - *"Seventy weeks are determined, for your people and for your holy city, to finish the transgression, to make an end of sins, to make reconciliation for iniquity, to bring in everlasting righteousness, to seal up vision and prophecy, And to anoint the Most Holy."*

Luke 15:20 - *"And he arose and came to his father. But when he was still a great way off, his father saw him and had compassion, and ran and fell on his neck and kissed him."*

Romans 5:10-11 – *"For if when we were enemies we were reconciled to God through the death of His Son, much more, having been reconciled, we shall be saved by His life. And not only that, but we also rejoice in God through our Lord Jesus Christ, through whom we have now received the reconciliation."*

Ephesians 2:14-16 – *"For He Himself is our peace, who has made both one, and has broken down the middle wall of separation, having abolished in His flesh the enmity, that is, the law of commandments contained in ordinances, so as to create in Himself* **one new man** *from the two, thus making peace, and that He might reconcile them both to God in one body through the cross, thereby putting to death the enmity."*

Hebrews 2:17 – *"Therefore, in all things He had to be made like His brethren, that He might be a merciful and faithful High Priest in things pertaining to God, to make propitiation for the sins of the people."*

Reconciliation also means to re-establish a fractured relationship. We know that God has called all races and cultures to be part of His kingdom and each one is needed to get the job of advancing His kingdom into every area of the world. There are several stories of fractured relationships that need to be re-established. The Prodigal Son and his father (Luke 15), Saul and David, (I Samuel 18), Hosea and Gomer, Esau and Jacob (Genesis 33), and Joseph and his brothers.

Let's first look at Esau and Jacob. In Gen 25-27, it tells the story of Isaac and Rebekah having twin sons. The older son was Esau and the younger son was Jacob. As the story goes Jacob had Esau sell him his birth right as the oldest for a bowl of stew. In Genesis 25:28, it says, "And Isaac loved Esau because he ate of his game, but Rebekah loved Jacob. Now Jacob cooked a stew; and Esau came in from the field, and he was weary. And Esau said to Jacob, "Please feed me with that same red stew, for I am weary." Therefore his name was called Edom. But Jacob said, "Sell me your birthright as of this day." And Esau said, "Look, I am about to die; so what is this birthright to me?" Then Jacob said, "Swear to me as of this day." So he swore to him, and sold his birthright to Jacob. And Jacob gave Esau bread and stew of lentils; then he ate and drank, arose, and went his way. Thus Esau despised his birthright. I believe the fight is not so much for the family's material wealth than it is for the blessing that was to be passed on. The blessing that they wanted was the blessing that Abraham conferred unto Isaac. Usually the father's blessing would be passed on to the oldest child. Esau was the heir to receive the blessings; however, if you go back to Genesis 25:21-23 it says, 'Now Isaac pleaded with the LORD for his wife, because she was barren; and the LORD granted his plea, and Rebekah, his wife, conceived. But the children struggled together within her; and she said, "If all is well, why am I like this?" So she went to inquire of the LORD. And the LORD said to her: "Two nations are in your womb, two peoples shall be separated from your body; one people shall be stronger than the other, And the older shall serve the younger."

This was a prophetic word that states that Jacob was the chosen one to receive the birthright. Maybe Isaac didn't believe this word or because of his love for Esau he tried to secretly pass it on to him without the rest of the family knowing. Both Isaac and Rebekah were guilty of another sin, the sin of showing favoritism towards their children. In chapter 25 we're told that Isaac loved Esau, the hunter, the man's man, but Rebekah loved Jacob, the quieter, more refined character. In showing favoritism toward Esau and trying to bless him in secret, Isaac fails to take leadership in his family; he fails to bring his family together; and he fails to listen to what God is really saying. Rebekah on the other hand has her own plan and plot to have Jacob receive the blessing and it is allowed to work. Both Isaac and Rebekah understand that having the blessing that God gave to Abraham was very precious and valuable and wanted their favorite son to have it. This situation caused much division and hatred between the brothers. But in Genesis 33:1-4, "Now Jacob lifted his eyes and looked, and there, Esau was coming, and with him were four hundred men. So he divided the children among Leah, Rachel, and the two maidservants. And he put the maidservants and their children in front, Leah and her children behind, and Rachel and Joseph last. Then he crossed over before them and bowed himself to the ground seven times, until he came near to his brother. But Esau ran to meet him, and embraced him, and fell on his neck and kissed him, and they wept. Despite all that had gone seemly wrong in their relationship these two men allowed God to move on their hearts and they reconciled.

The last story of reconciliation I want to look at is the story of Joseph and his brothers. This is one of the most powerful stories of reconciliation in the Bible. And the Lord uses it to give us a model of how we are to walk in the spirit of reconciliation being the Ministers of Reconciliation that we are called to be in

Him. In Genesis 37-50, it tells the story of Jacob's favorite son Joseph who wore the coat of many colors. The story of Joseph helps get over any feelings of resent by allowing the power of God's love, grace and truth to bring reconciliation between any two opposing parties. Learning how to forgive others helps free us from the destructive tendency that comes from being critical, angry, and fearful. Joseph's brothers were afraid that Joseph was going to be angry with them and possibly kill them. When we don't reconcile with people we can open the door for anger, resentment, bitterness, jealousy, envy, fear, estrangement, bickering, back-biting, divisions, factions, slander, rejection and much more.

This story is about Joseph's brothers being jealous of Joseph, because he was his father's favorite but he also told them he had dreams of him being superior to them and that they would bow down to him. Now Joseph had a dream, and he told it to his brothers; and they hated him even more. So he said to them, "Please hear this dream which I have dreamed: "There we were, binding sheaves in the field. Then behold, my sheaf arose and also stood upright; and indeed your sheaves stood all around and bowed down to my sheaf." And his brothers said to him, "Shall you indeed reign over us? Or shall you indeed have dominion over us?" So they hated him even more for his dreams and for his words (Genesis 37:5-8).

The brothers decided not to kill him but to put him in a pit until they decided what they would do to him. They decided to sell him into slavery which caused a long list of tragic things to happen in Joseph's life.

But it doesn't end there, Joseph through some events that only God could orchestrate became the Prime Minister in Egypt. He was the second most powerful man in their world at that time. He brings a major solution to the nation regarding provisions during a seven year drought. He actually comes up with (by the power of God) a 14-year plan to save the nation. Everyone in the world at that time had to come to him for food, including his brothers. When he realizes who his brothers were he took them through some things to see if they had changed their hearts in anyway. Finally after several meetings with them he wept and let them know his identity. Then Joseph could not restrain himself before all those who stood by him, and he cried out, "Make everyone go out from me!" So no one stood with him while Joseph made himself known to his brothers. And he wept aloud, and the Egyptians and the house of Pharaoh heard it. Then Joseph said to his brothers, "I am Joseph; does my father still live?" But his brothers could not answer him, for they were dismayed in his presence. And Joseph said to his brothers, *"Please come near to me."* So they came near. Then he said: "I am Joseph your brother, whom you sold into Egypt. (Genesis 45:1-4)

Joseph then tells them that they did not send him to Egypt, but that God had. Then in Genesis, 45:5, it says, He begins to take steps toward reconciliation with his brothers. Verse 7-8: *"And God sent me before you to preserve a posterity for you in the earth, and to save your lives by a great deliverance." So now it was not you who sent me here, but God; and He has made me a father to Pharaoh, and lord of all his house, and a ruler throughout all the land of Egypt.*

Reconciliation at its greatest; (Genesis 45:14-15) Then he fell on his brother Benjamin's neck and wept, and Benjamin wept on his neck. Moreover, he kissed all his brothers and wept over them, and after that his brothers talked with him. True godly, people know how to practice the ministry of reconciliation in the loving and kind way that Jesus does. There are times when people don't even deserve our forgiveness but because of the mercy of God they offer it. Jesus on the cross said Father forgive them for they know not what they are doing. (Luke 23:43) And they divided His garments and cast lots. Joseph like Jesus demonstrates great compassion and reconciles with his fearful brothers. They were still fearful when their father Jacob died. In Genesis 50:16-21, we find they sent messengers to Joseph, saying, *"Before your father died he commanded, saying, 'Thus you shall say to Joseph: "I beg you, please forgive the trespass of your brothers and their sin; for they did evil to you." 'Now, please, forgive the trespass of the servants of the God of your father." And Joseph wept when they spoke to him. Then his brothers also went and fell down before his face, and they said, "Behold, we are your servants." Joseph said to them, "Do not be afraid, for am I in the place of God? "**But as for you, you meant evil against me; but God meant it for good, in order to bring it about as it is this day, to save many people alive.** "Now therefore, do not be afraid; I will provide for you and your little ones."* And he comforted them and spoke kindly to them.

People who are truly, genuinely humble, contrite, and repentant will confess their sins so that everyone involved can be restored. When a person is full of pride they remain stubborn and resistant to acknowledge their sins. Until people are willing to take full responsibility for the sins they commit they will not be able to allow God's healing and cleansing power to clear their conscience. We must check out our motives because motives are very important to God. We must have pure motives and be willing to allow God to cleanse our minds, wills, and emotions in order to please Him. When people decide not to forgive they fail to submit their will, emotions, and mind to the Lord's control. It doesn't mean that God will not use them but it means that He can't fully use them to advance in certain areas. Another aspect of the Joseph anointing is the anointing to reconcile and forgive one another. The entire plan of God was to use Joseph to save a nation of people and to also display the love of Jesus Christ through him just as He wants to do through us! Mar 2:10 "But that you may know that the Son of Man has power on earth to forgive sins"—He said to the paralytic,

Over the years I've been in many racial and culture reconciliation meetings that involved many different people. When I first began to be involved in these types of meetings I really didn't understand what was happening. I had to be taught about identification repentance/reconciliation. This means that I can stand on behalf of any group that I represent. For example, I'm a mother of two children, so I can stand on behalf of mothers. I'm a leader in the body of Christ, so I can stand and represent leaders. I'm an African-American, so I can stand and represent African-Americans. I'm an intercessor, so I can stand on behalf of intercessors. I also have Native American blood, so I can stand on behalf of Natives, etc. This was knowledge that was needed to understand what was happening at these meetings. So, as I was attending the different meetings of race and culture, reconciliation was taking place and I would be asked to stand on behalf of the African slaves who were in America. At first I was a little offended and would think I'm not a slave and I've never been a slave so stop trying to take me back into bondage. But as I gained understanding, I began to learn I was standing on behalf of my ancestors who were victims of slavery. While standing for my African ancestors, who were slaves, I was able to receive the repentance of persons who wanted to be forgiven for the part that their ancestors may have played in slavery. I was also able to offer repentance to persons who the slaves may have retaliated against. In the early to mid-2000's I began to experience some deep deliverance at these types of meetings. I must have participated in hundreds of these types of meetings; some were planned and others were spontaneous. There were some that people were just going through the act and checking their repentance box because someone told them they needed to do this. But there were some meetings that were very powerful and heartfelt that I know the hand of the Lord had orchestrated them. The following list is not in chronological order:

Waycross, GA

One of the purest reconciliation meetings that I was in was held in Waycross, Georgia. The city of Waycross was named because it was considered at one time to be the place that the way of the cross of Jesus Christ was lived. The church where we held a prayer, praise and worship gathering was founded by one of the former Azusa Street participants host in California by William Seymour. The Holy Spirit broke in on our meeting and we had a good representation of different races and cultures. We had Jews, African-Americans, Africans, Caucasians, Hispanics, older people, and young people. Both a female and a male Caucasian couple both had grandfathers that were former slave owners. All of us stood in the front of the church and it began with everyone repenting to the Jews. The Bible says the Jew first, for all the things our nation has done against them. Earlier that day there had been a reconciliation meeting with the Native Americans – the nation host people. It was clear that God had set this day aside to be a day of reconciliation for all his people present. The African person repented to the African-American person for their part in slavery (which I will discuss later in this chapter). Each group further repented to each other for various things but there was something that stood out and was a marked difference to me. The female Caucasian came to me as I stood on behalf of the African-American slaves, and said "I want to repent to you woman to woman." I thought, this is a new one, and she said, "I want you to forgive the Caucasian women for hating you as African-American slave women; we hated you because at night our husbands wanted to be with you rather than us. And we also hated you and we hated the offspring that came out of that relationship. So we would separate you and send your children who looked like our husbands away as though it never happened." And we had a Caucasian man repent on behalf of what the male slave owners did to both the Caucasian family and the African-American family. Also, what the slave owners had done to the slaves' mentality, socially, and economically. Something deep in my soul broke off of me. It was if I had an unknown wound deep in my soul that was very painful and all of a sudden it was miraculously healed. The same man said I want to restore your dignity back to you. Praise the Lord what a powerful meeting. As an African-American I repented to the Caucasians for the way the African-Americans retaliated. I said we didn't know how to react to all that was done to us, so we retaliated by causing other cultures pain through murder, rape, and much more.

Simpsonwoods Retreat Center

At this conference we hosted leaders from 75 nations.

These were prayer meetings pertaining to a large government meeting in our area. As we were praying one day the Holy Spirit broke in on us and said we needed to reconcile the nations that were represented there. There were many races and cultures represented there and the different cultures began speaking what was in their hearts and repenting to each other. What stood out about this meeting was there was a Native Chief from Canada there and he wanted to repent to the African-Americans because the Natives were upset thinking that when the slaves got their freedom; that in turn the African-Americans would help them get their true freedom. I had never heard anything like this before but when I heard it I knew it was valid. So I proceeded to repent to the Native Americans for not helping them obtain their freedom as well. When the power of God is operating at one of these meetings you don't have time to intellectualize or rationalize what is happening. If someone has an offense, Act 24:16 says *"This being so, I myself always strive to have a conscience without offense toward God and men then help release your brother."*

While at this same conference I noticed two women from Africa who were very standoffish from me. I was one of the leaders helping lead the administrative portion of this conference. This meant that I had to interact with just about every participant in the conference. My interaction with these two ladies was awkward and cold. I was trying to understand naturally and spiritually what was between us. I prayed and asked the Lord what was going on, why are we not connecting as we should? I didn't get an immediate answer from the Lord. On one day we had planned a shopping outing for the leaders that wanted to go and buy some American-made things while in our country. I noticed that the two African women did not go and neither did I. I was longing for a quiet moment to get some rest from serving everyone. My position had me getting up very early every morning and staying up late every night. So I was longing for a moment to recoup and a nap was the cure. Well, just as I had arrived to my room, laid my head on the pillow and closed my weary eyes; I heard the Lord say, "You need to go and repent to those African women." I said huh? And I heard Him say again "You need to go and repent to those African women." I knew it was the Lord, so I got up and as I was putting on my shoes the Lord further said, "Take some money with you and give them a peace offering. At that moment one of my trusted intercessor friends called and I told them what the Lord had said and they brought confirmation and asked me to take money on their behalf as well.

So, I went down the stairs to their room not knowing what I was going to repent about and as I knocked on their door the Lord said, "Repent for not helping them when they came to the USA and not going back to try to rescue them out of their impoverished state in Africa." I thought what? You see at this time in my life I had not considered the plight of Africans in Africa. Let alone that they were my ancestors or connected to me in any way at all. But God changed all that. When I went in I asked how they were doing they said very coldly everything was going fine. I then began to tell them why I was there. I said that I wanted to repent to them on behalf of the African-Americans because of how we have treated them when they have come to America. How we have not supported them, how we have been ashamed of them, and how we have discarded them as if they were not connected to us. I said part of us not acknowledging them was us trying to forget where we came from and that we didn't want to be associated with Africans that we thought lived in a jungle. I asked forgiveness for us as African-Americans acting as if we were better or more superior to the Africans.

One of the ladies replied and said we have been told not to trust any African-American people while in the USA because you would lie to us. Here it is again the enemy trying to keep people separated from each other. So they accepted my repentance and began to repent to me. She said we must also ask you to forgive us. We thought you were over here in the USA living in the lap of luxury and did not realize the pain and suffering that you were going through during slavery. But, also, I must ask you to forgive us for our younger brother Joseph, who we sold into slavery, so please forgive us for what we have done to you. She said we release you Joseph into your wealth so you can come home and save our nations. Oh my goodness, this was another time when I experienced a deep unknown wound in my soul be healed and delivered. We all wept uncontrollably and accepted each other's forgiveness. In a meeting at the same conference, a Canadian Prophet (who didn't know what had happened) prophesied and said God is sending you to the Continent of Africa, and you shall visit many nations there, both large and small, and you will take these nations into the throne room of Heaven before the Father's Throne and receive justice on their behalf. Then he went and put money in my hands and said this is a sign that money will not be an issue.

HAPN Oklahoma

I was at an HAPN (Heartland Apostolic Prayer Network) meeting where I am the National Multicultural Affairs Leader. During that meeting, the leader for Israel Rabbi Curt Landry, being led by the Holy Spirit called up all the African-American people and there were about five of us out of about 500 people. He began to repent and said "I want to repent to you on behalf of my ancestor King David for what he did to your ancestor Obed Edom. At that moment time stopped for me, what does Obed Edom have to do with us? Well, he further said something to the effect that King David got mad at God for what He did to Uzzah (2 Samuel 6:6), by killing him for touching the Ark of the Covenant. David was angry with God and sent the Ark to Obed Edom's house with the thought that if the Lord kills the African Obed Edom it is no big deal. Wow! You must catch the rest of the story. (2 Samuel 6:9-12) *David was afraid of the LORD that day; and he said, "How can the ark of the LORD come to me?" So David would not move the ark of the LORD with him into the City of David; but David took it aside into the house of Obed-Edom the Gittite. The ark of the LORD remained in the house of Obed-Edom the Gittite three months. And the LORD blessed Obed-Edom and all his household. Now it was told King David, saying, "The LORD has blessed the house of Obed-Edom and all that belongs to him, because of the ark of God." So David went and brought up the ark of God from the house of Obed-Edom to the City of David with gladness.*

As the story goes when King David was told about how the Obed-Edom house was blessed and none of them were killed, King David wanted the Ark back. Rabbi Landry also said many other things, but this was another one of the major healings and deliverances I received through reconciliation.

Jerusalem, Israel

I was on a wonderful prayer journey in Jerusalem, Israel. I was part of another ministry who had an assignment to take a Team of twenty-four Elders and go to very strategic locations in

Israel and declare Scriptures out of Revelation regarding the 24 praising and worshipping God around His throne. In Revelation 4:4, it says *"Around the throne were twenty-four thrones, and on the thrones I saw twenty-four elders sitting, clothed in white robes; and they had crowns of gold on their heads."* Then in Revelation 4:10-11, *"the twenty-four elders fall down before Him who sits on the throne and worship Him who lives forever and ever, and cast their crowns before the throne, saying: "You are worthy, O Lord, To receive glory and honor and power; For You created all things, And by Your will they exist and were created." We were doing this as a prophetic act for the presence of God to come to Israel in a greater way and for souls to be saved."*

While on the trip I met a wonderful young woman who became my friend. After we would finish our God-given assignments for the day, our team would arrive back at the hotel. Esther and I would sit and talk trying to get to know each other better. One night, out-of-the-blue, Esther who has a mixed nationality asked why is that black people now want to be called African-Americans. It seemed like a fairly simple question but it had quite a complicated answer. She further explained other cultures are not asking to be called Asian-American, Latin-American, etc. I answered her and said the African-American people have been a people of lost identity. Many people have called us various names such as colored, Negro, blacks and other not-so-nice names. Those names do not fully identify African-Americans. I told her personally one of my jobs in God's kingdom is to help restore the African-American people's identity. The name Africa connects us to our homeland of Africa. America identifies us as American citizens. I said many people do not understand what the big deal is because they have never had their identity stolen and they haven't had to live by names that other people have given them. Esther then said to me, with tears in her eyes, I didn't realize African-American people's history until I saw the movie "The Help" and until I read "To Kill a Mocking Bird." She said it was wrong on so many levels, "we tore apart your families and treated you like animals." We both began to weep; this reconciliation was taking on such a different dimension. I thought I was totally delivered from the bondage and effects of racism, slavery and the like. I interjected that people think we can offer repentance once and it is done with. She said that's why we must keep repenting because there were so many levels of wrongdoings that took place. She continued and said to call a group of people less than human is unbelievable, "I am so sorry for all we have done to your people. Please forgive us." With many tears I accepted the repentance and released her and everyone she represented from the wrong that had been done. I also asked for forgiveness for the way the African-Americans wrongfully retaliated. This was another game changer because it was the first repentance offered to me on Israel soil. We both got powerfully delivered and set free on our homeland territory. We believe that our Lord and Savior Jesus Christ had set this up as an appointed time for us to move forward to fulfill our destiny! God is a god of reconciliation and has given us all the Ministry of Reconciliation to go forth and to heal the nations. Let us all begin to practice this powerful ministry and watch people get free. Amen!

Chapter Thirteen

Embracing Our Jewish Heritage

Holidays are celebrations that nations of people observe around the world honoring people, places, and events. Every culture, tribe and nation has its own sets of holidays celebrated at certain times of the year. They are usually in memory of some significant political event, birthdays of nation leaders and, most often, they are connected to some religious belief or superstition acknowledged by the nation. They are usually events which are observed by a group of specific people.

Our eternal God in the Holy Bible has instituted only seven major holidays for His people. These holidays are referred to throughout the Bible both in the Old and New Testament. These can be found in Leviticus, the 23rd chapter. They are referred to as "the feasts of the Lord," which means they are His holidays. The word feast means appointed times. These are appointed times that God has called His people to celebrate and recall a part of Israel's history. Many times they are referred to as a "holy convocations" which means these are times that God and His people meet for holy purposes. The Jewish people have many holidays but we will refer to the seven in Leviticus 23 as the most important and then we will only focus on three of the major ones. (Leviticus 23:1) *And the LORD spoke to Moses, saying, 2)*

"Speak to the children of Israel, and say to them: 'The feasts of the LORD, which you shall proclaim [to be] holy convocations, these [are] My feasts. 3) 'Six days shall work be done, but the seventh day [is] a Sabbath of solemn rest, a holy convocation. You shall do no work [on it]; it [is] the Sabbath of the LORD in all your dwellings. 4) 'These [are] the feasts of the LORD, holy convocations which you shall proclaim at their appointed times. 5) 'On the fourteenth [day] of the first month at twilight [is] the LORD's Passover. 6) 'And on the fifteenth day of the same month [is] the Feast of Unleavened Bread to the LORD; seven days you must eat unleavened bread. 7) 'On the first day you shall have a holy convocation; you shall do no customary work on it. 8) 'But you shall offer an offering made by fire to the LORD for seven days. The seventh day [shall be] a holy convocation; you shall do no customary work [on it]. 9) And the LORD spoke to Moses, saying, and through verse 44.

During these holidays the Jews would stop all regular work and be devoted totally to these celebrations. There would be specific types of meals with portions set aside for the priests and the rest would be given and gathered at the temple for worship. They would be celebrated with much thanksgiving, worship, and joyous feasting which commemorated significant events in Israel's history as God's covenant people. When I first began hearing about the feast I would get them all confused because some may have been called two or three different names. The three major feasts that we will discuss in this book is Passover, Pentecost, and Tabernacles. These are the three major feasts when all the Israelites were required to travel to Jerusalem to participate in the events and the men were to present themselves to the Lord. It is in Exodus 23:14 *"Three times you shall keep a feast to Me in the year: 15) "You shall keep the Feast of Unleavened Bread (you shall eat unleavened bread seven days, as I commanded you, at the time appointed in the month of Abib, for in it you came out of Egypt; none shall appear before Me empty); 16) "and the Feast of Harvest, the Firstfruits of your labors which you have sown in the field; and the Feast of Ingathering at the end of the year, when you have gathered in [the fruit of] your labors from the field. 17) "Three times in the year all your males shall appear before the Lord GOD. 18) "You shall not offer the blood of My sacrifice with leavened bread; nor shall the fat of My sacrifice remain until morning. 19) "The first of the Firstfruits of your land you shall bring into the house of the LORD your God. You shall not boil a young goat in its mother's milk.*

1. PASSOVER - Pesach Observed in spring

> *Verse 5: On the fourteenth day of the first month at twilight is the Lord's Passover.*

2. FEAST OF UNLEAVENED BREAD - Observed in Spring

> *Verse 6: And on the fifteenth day of the same month is the Feast of Unleavened Bread to the Lord; seven days you must eat unleavened bread.*

> *Verse 7: On the first day you shall have a holy convocation; you shall do no customary work on it.*

> *Verse 8: But you shall offer an offering made by fire to the Lord for seven days. The seventh day shall be a holy convocation; you shall do no customary work on it.' "*

> *Verse 9: And the Lord spoke to Moses, saying,*

3. FEAST OF FIRSTFRUITS - Observed in Spring

Verse 10: "Speak to the children of Israel, and say to them: 'When you come into the land which I give to you, and reap its harvest, then you shall bring a sheaf of the Firstfruits of your harvest to the priest.

Verse11: He shall wave the sheaf before the Lord, to be accepted on your behalf; on the day after the Sabbath the priest shall wave it.

Verse 12: And you shall offer on that day, when you wave the sheaf, a male lamb of the first year, without blemish, as a burnt offering to the Lord.

Verse 13: Its grain offering shall be two-tenths of an ephah of fine flour mixed with oil, an offering made by fire to the Lord, for a sweet aroma; and its drink offering shall be of wine, one-fourth of him.

Verse 14: You shall eat neither bread nor parched grain nor fresh grain until the same day that you have brought an offering to your God; it shall be a statute forever throughout your generations in all your dwellings.

4. PENTECOST - FEAST OF PENTECOST (WEEKS) is connected to Shavout - Observed in Spring

Verse 15: 'And you shall count for yourselves from the day after the Sabbath, from the day that you brought the sheaf of the wave offering: seven Sabbaths shall be completed.

Verse16: Count fifty days to the day after the seventh Sabbath; then you shall offer a new grain offering to the Lord.

Verse 17: You shall bring from your dwellings two wave loaves of two-tenths of an ephah. They shall be of fine flour; they shall be baked with leaven. They are the Firstfruits to the Lord.

Verse18: And you shall offer with the bread seven lambs of the first year, without blemish, one young bull, and two rams. They shall be as a burnt offering to the Lord, with their grain offering and their drink offerings, an offering made by fire for a sweet aroma to the Lord.

Verse 19: Then you shall sacrifice one kid of the goats as a sin offering, and two male lambs of the first year as a sacrifice of a peace offering.

Verse 20: The priest shall wave them with the bread of the Firstfruits as a wave offering before the Lord, with the two lambs. They shall be holy to the Lord for the priest.

Verse 21: And you shall proclaim on the same day that it is a holy convocation to you. You shall do no customary work on it. It shall be a statute forever in all your dwellings throughout your generations.

Verse 22: 'When you reap the harvest of your land, you shall not wholly reap the corners of your field when you reap, nor shall you gather any gleaning from your harvest. You shall leave them for the poor and for the stranger: I am the Lord your God.' "

5. FEAST OF TRUMPETS - Rosh Hoshanah -Jewish New Year - Observed in the Fall

Verse 23: Then the Lord spoke to Moses, saying,

Verse 24: "Speak to the children of Israel, saying: 'In the seventh month, on the first day of the month, you shall have a sabbath-rest, a memorial of blowing of trumpets, a holy convocation.

Verse 25:You shall do no customary work on it; and you shall offer an offering made by fire to the Lord.' "

6. DAY OF ATONEMENT - Yom Kippur - Observed in the Fall

Verse 26: And the Lord spoke to Moses, saying:

Verse 27: "Also the tenth day of this seventh month shall be the Day of Atonement. It shall be a holy convocation for you; you shall afflict your souls, and offer an offering made by fire to the Lord.

Verse 28: And you shall do no work on that same day, for it is the Day of Atonement, to make atonement for you before the Lord your God.

Verse 29: For any person who is not afflicted in soul on that same day shall be cut off from his people. 30 And any person who does any work on that same day, that person I will destroy from among his people.

Verse 31: You shall do no manner of work; it shall be a statute forever throughout your generations in all your dwellings.

Verse 32: It shall be to you a sabbath of solemn rest, and you shall afflict your souls; on the ninth day of the month at evening, from evening to evening, you shall celebrate your sabbath."

7. FEAST OF TABERNACLES - Sukkot, Feast of Booths, Feast of Ingathering - Observed in Fall

Verse 33: Then the Lord spoke to Moses, saying,

Verse 34: "Speak to the children of Israel, saying: 'The fifteenth day of this seventh month shall be the Feast of Tabernacles for seven days to the Lord.

Verse 35: On the first day there shall be a holy convocation. You shall do no customary work on it.

Verse 36: For seven days you shall offer an offering made by fire to the Lord. On the eighth day you shall have a holy convocation, and you shall offer an offering made by fire to the Lord. It is a sacred assembly, and you shall do no customary work on it.

Verse 37: These are the feasts of the Lord which you shall proclaim to be holy convocations, to offer an offering made by fire to the Lord, a burnt offering and a grain offering, a sacrifice and drink offerings, everything on its day--

Verse 38: besides the Sabbaths of the Lord, besides your gifts, besides all your vows, and besides all your freewill offerings which you give to the Lord.

Verse 39: 'Also on the fifteenth day of the seventh month, when you have gathered in the fruit of the land, you shall keep the feast of the Lord for seven days; on the first day there shall be a Sabbath-rest, and on the eighth day a Sabbath-rest.

Verse 40: And you shall take for yourselves on the first day the fruit of beautiful trees, branches of palm trees, the boughs of leafy trees, and willows of the brook; and you shall rejoice before the Lord your God for seven days.

Verse 41: You shall keep it as a feast to the Lord for seven days in the year. It shall be a statute forever in your generations. You shall celebrate it in the seventh month.

Verse 42: You shall dwell in booths for seven days. All who are native Israelites shall dwell in booths,

Verse 43: that your generations may know that I made the children of Israel dwell in booths when I brought them out of the land of Egypt: I am the Lord your God.'
"

Verse 44: So Moses declared to the children of Israel the feasts of the Lord.

For a more in-depth study you can seek out other materials to give you a full blown description of how to celebrate each. The purpose of this information is to introduce the reader to the need for believers and Keturah's children to learn about their heritage. I believe we should celebrate what God wants us to celebrate to bring His glory and His fullest blessing into our lives. In this book I wanted to bring awareness to three main holidays: Passover, Pentecost, and Tabernacles.

Passover

The Jewish people had lived in bondage for more than 400 years being enslaved by the Egyptians. All the favor that Joseph had with the Pharaoh had disappeared and the Israelites found themselves in slavery. But, the time had come for God to deliver them from their slavery. In Exodus 2:23-25 it says, *"Now it happened in the process of time that the king of Egypt died. Then the children of Israel groaned because of the bondage, and they cried out; and their cry came up to God because of the bondage. 24) So God heard their groaning, and God remembered His covenant with Abraham, with Isaac, and with Jacob. 25) And God looked upon the children of Israel, and God acknowledged [them].*

And then in Exodus 3:7-9, *"And the LORD said: "I have surely seen the oppression of My people who [are] in Egypt, and have heard their cry because of their taskmasters, for I know their sorrows. 8) "So I have come down to deliver them out of the hand of the Egyptians, and to bring them up from that land to a good and large land, to a land flowing with milk and honey, to the place of the Canaanites and the Hittites and the Amorites and the Perizzites and the Hivites and the Jebusites. 9) "Now therefore, behold, the cry of the children of Israel has come to Me, and I have also seen the oppression with which the Egyptians oppress them.*

And in Exodus 6:6, *"Therefore, say to the children of Israel: 'I [am] the LORD; I will bring you out from under the burdens of the Egyptians, I will rescue you from their bondage, and I will redeem you with an outstretched arm and with great judgments.*

God had decided by using all type of signs and wonders that He was going to set His people free. He promised the children of Israel and its leader Moses that He was going to bring them out of bondage of slavery with a strong hand. Moses had gone to Pharaoh and requested that he would release the children of Israel and he refused. So over a period of nine months God sent

10 plagues upon the Egyptians to break Pharaoh's will. They were:

1.   The Nile River turned into blood (Exodus 7:14-25)

2.   He sent frogs (Exodus 8:1-15)

3.   He sent an infestation of lice (Exodus 8:16-19)

4.   He sent swarms of flies (Exodus 8:20-32)

5.   He sent diseases (Exodus 9:1-7)

6.   He sent boils and sores upon everyone (Exodus 9:8-12)

7.   Hail storms that destroyed crops (Exodus 9:13-35)

8.   He sent swarm of locust (Exodus 10:1-20)

9.   He sent thick darkness for 3 days (Exodus 10:21-29)

10.   The Egyptians firstborn were destroyed by the death Angel sent by God (Exodus 11:1-12:30)

All of these plagues addressed and were attached to one of the gods that the Egyptians worshipped. In all the plagues that were sent, the Israelites where protected and not harmed at all. At the 10th plague, God gave some specific instructions on how they should protect themselves against the death Angel in Exodus 11. Their protection from this plague would come from their acts of obedience to God's instruction. The final judgment was for the death Angel to kill every first born in the country. But God always has a way out for His people. Refer to I Corinthians 10:13, *"No temptation has overtaken you except such as is common to man; but God [is] faithful, who will not allow you to be tempted beyond what you are able, but with the temptation will also make the way of escape, that you may be able to bear [it]."*

The children of Israel were to select a year-old male lamb that was perfect without any blemish or flaw. On the 10th day of the Hebrew, month of Nisan, it was to be taken out from the flock and kept in the house with the family until the 14th day of the month. They were to become personally attached to their lamb so that it wouldn't be just another lamb, but this lamb would become their lamb. The lamb would become a part of the family. This would show them the costly nature of their sacrifice. It was their lamb that they had grown to love that was going to be sacrificed for their sins. They were to kill the lamb in public and take the blood and apply it to their doorpost at their home as a sign of their faith in the Lord. This would cause the death Angel to pass over their house. And this is how the Lord instituted Passover as a night to remember the Lord allowing the death Angel to Passover them and for Him bringing them out of Egypt.

Passover Service

There are very meaningful parts to a Passover Service that I will not discuss in detail in this book. You can search for material in your local bookstore or go online to query the step-by-step on how to celebrate Passover. I will give you a very high level overview here. God commands us to celebrate the Passover as a memorial forever in Exodus 12:14: *'So this day shall be to you a memorial; and you shall keep it as a feast to the LORD throughout your generations. You shall keep it as a feast by an everlasting ordinance.* He also requires us to have a service. Exodus 12:25 says, "It will come to pass when you come to the land which the LORD will give you, just as He promised, that

177

you shall keep this service. At the service there is a major meal called the Seder, which means order. So there is a certain order in which everything is done and everything has a specific meaning relating to the Israelites history. There are Scripture readings, prayers, symbolic foods, and songs in the Passover Service. There is a lamb, wine, matzoth crackers (unleavened bread), and bitter herbs that all have meaning. And the Exodus story of Passover is rehearsed and told from generation to generation (Exodus 12).

PENTECOST - Feast of Weeks, also known as Shavuot

Leviticus 23:15 - *'And you shall count for yourselves from the day after the Sabbath, from the day that you brought the sheaf of the wave offering: seven Sabbaths shall be completed.*

16) 'Count fifty days to the day after the seventh Sabbath; then you shall offer a new grain offering to the LORD.

Acts 2:1 - *When the Day of Pentecost had fully come, they were all with one accord in one place.*

Acts 2:2 - *And suddenly there came a sound from heaven, as of a rushing mighty wind, and it filled the whole house where they were sitting.*

Acts 2:3 - *Then there appeared to them divided tongues, as of fire, and one sat upon each of them.*

Acts 2:4 - *And they were all filled with the Holy Spirit and began to speak with other tongues, as the Spirit gave them utterance.*

As I said before some of the Lord's Holidays have several names with several meanings and each gives a significant understanding of the holiday. The first name for this feast is Shavuot, which means "weeks," in Hebrew. Then there is "Feast of Weeks" to represent the seven weeks that were counted from the Feast of First Fruits. It is also called "the Day of Firstfruits" because it was marked as the start of the summer wheat harvest. Pentecost is the meaning of Shavuot in Greek language that means fiftieth. This Feast is observed most times in late May or early June. In Leviticus 23:15-21 and in Numbers 28:26-31, it tells us how we must celebrate. In Deuteronomy 16:9-12, it spells out what an individual is required to offer.

Deuteronomy 16:9 - *"You shall count seven weeks for yourself; begin to count the seven weeks from the time you begin to put the sickle to the grain.*

Deuteronomy 16:10 - *"Then you shall keep the Feast of Weeks to the LORD your God with the tribute of a freewill offering from your hand, which you shall give as the LORD your God blesses you.*

Deuteronomy 16:11 - *"You shall rejoice before the LORD your God, you and your son and your daughter, your male servant and your female servant, the Levite who is within your gates, the stranger and the fatherless and the widow who are among you, at the place where the LORD your God chooses to make His name abide.*

Deuteronomy 16:12 - *"And you shall remember that you were a slave in Egypt, and you shall be careful to observe these statutes.*

We are instructed by the Lord to bring a freewill offering, rejoice before the Lord and to remember that HE brought us out of Egyptian slavery. Something that I have noticed about the Feast of the Lord is that all, except one, are for celebrating, having fun, and enjoying the Lord. That's why some kingdom people don't have any strength because they have only taught us to be sad and somber before the Lord. But the Bible says weeping may endure for a night and joy comes in the morning. The joy of the Lord is my strength! So if the enemy can keep you sad and pitiful he's got your strength. I have always told our church that there are too many joys - be glad, rejoice, enjoy, be happy! Happiness is in the Bible, and not for me to be a poor pitiful, crying all the time, broke down Christian! The Feast will help break the power of the enemy off of you and you will realize what a great and mighty God we serve and that we are a blessed people. There are three major blessings associated with Pentecost-Shavuot. The **first** blessing is for our provision. At Pentecost we are celebrating God's blessings of abundant provisions. Yes, material blessing. In the Old Testament most of the people of Israel were farmers who planted crops and expected a harvest. As a little sweet girl in Texas my grandparents and parents did a little farming/gardening. They taught us to diligently prepare the ground by digging it up and removing weeds in order to plant. The children of Israel did the same thing, but on a much larger scale. After planting they knew that they had no ability to cause the rain to come or the Earth to produce. So they had to trust God for rain and a harvest of whatever crop planted. Thus, they expected God to bless them with great harvests which He would and they would give burnt offerings, grain offerings, drink offerings, sin offerings, fellowship offerings and freewill offerings because God had blessed them during the harvest season. So they had an enormous amount of provisions given by the Lord! The **second** blessing is that supernatural revelation would come during this season. It was the day that the Lord opened up the heavens and released His word. This is said to be the time that God gave Moses the Law at Mt. Sinai. The **third** blessing is that of power.

Acts 2:1 – *"When the Day of Pentecost had fully come, they were all with one accord in one place.*

Acts 2:2 – *"And suddenly there came a sound from heaven,*

as of a rushing mighty wind, and it filled the whole house where they were sitting.

Acts 2:3 – *"Then there appeared to them divided tongues, as of fire, and one sat upon each of them.*

Acts 2:4 – *"And they were all filled with the Holy Spirit and began to speak with other tongues, as the Spirit gave them utterance."*

On Pentecost the power of God was released to the church, but that is not where it began. In Exodus 19:18 it says, *"And Mount Sinai was altogether on a smoke, because the LORD descended upon it in fire: and the smoke thereof ascended as the smoke of a furnace, and the whole mount quaked greatly"* God's power was released on Mount Sinai just as it was released on the day of Pentecost and He wants to release more of His power as we celebrate Pentecost today!

Service of Pentecost/Shavout

You can set a part a time to be with the Lord and reflect on His goodness and mercy. You can spend time with friends and family and enjoy praying, fellowship and food. One of the Jewish customs is to stay up all night and study the word, eat cheesecake and drink coffee. A small group of us did that and, oh my goodness, we have never experienced the presence of God like that before.

We studied the Book of Ruth and the Scripture came alive right before us. Now this is not something you have to do, but we wanted to experience it. Please do not turn these Feasts into another religious thing to do with a lot of meaningless rules to follow. It is a time to celebrate. Bring special offerings to your local church during this time. Spend a lot of time praising and thanking God for His goodness.

The spirit of poverty hates a spirit of praise, thanksgiving, and joy. Again, the Feast absolutely breaks the power of the enemy off a person's life.

Feast of Tabernacles-Sukkot-Ingathering

The final thing I want to talk about is the Feast of Tabernacles of Sukkot which means booth. This is the most festive and joyful Feasts of all. It is mentioned in the Book of John 7-9 as well as Leviticus 23:24-34.

Leviticus 23:24 - *"Speak to the children of Israel, saying: 'In the seventh month, on the first day of the month, you shall have a Sabbath-rest, a memorial of blowing of trumpets, a holy convocation.*

Leviticus 23:25 - *'You shall do no customary work on it; and you shall offer an offering made by fire to the LORD.'"*

Leviticus 23:26 – *"And the LORD spoke to Moses, saying:*

Leviticus 23:27 - *"Also the tenth day of this seventh month shall be the Day of Atonement. It shall be a holy convocation for you; you shall afflict your souls, and offer an offering made by fire to the LORD.*

Leviticus 23:28 - *"And you shall do no work on that same day, for it is the Day of Atonement, to make atonement for you before the LORD your God.*

Leviticus 23:29 - *"For any person who is not afflicted in soul on that same day shall be cut off from his people.*

Leviticus 23:30 - *"And any person who does any work on that same day, that person I will destroy from among his people.*

Leviticus 23:31 - *"You shall do no manner of work; it shall*

be a statute forever throughout your generations in all your
dwellings.

Leviticus 23:32 - *"It shall be to you a sabbath of solemn rest,*
and you shall afflict your souls; on the ninth day of the month
at evening, from evening to evening, you shall celebrate your
sabbath."

Leviticus 23:33 - *Then the LORD spoke to Moses, saying,*

Leviticus 23:34 - *"Speak to the children of Israel, saying:*
'The fifteenth day of this seventh month shall be the Feast of
Tabernacles for seven days to the LORD."

During this feast the children of Israel were to dwell in or live in tabernacles, shelters or temporary booths as a reminder of God's provision during the 40-year wilderness trip. It is celebrated with great joy and Feasting. They celebrate God's past goodness and all His provisions on the wilderness. It is a time for us to celebrate God's glory. It is a time to come into His presence. I had a recent trip to Israel and it was during the time of Feast of Tabernacles. I was surprised there were sukkots (temporary shelters) everywhere. People had them on their balconies, they had them in their backyards, in their driveways and any place they could erect one. The hotels had them by their pools, on the decks, and beside the hotel restaurant. They were in places I never thought they would be. The Jewish people understand it is a time to be with God. A time to tabernacle with Him and experience His presence.

When the children of Israel came out of Egypt they experienced His glory through the signs, wonders, and miracles. His glory is the tangible manifestation of His presence. Tabernacles remind us that God wants to be with His people. It helps us understand that God wants you to have fun celebrating and being with Him. It also reminds us that we should expect His glory to be with us, operating through us. Remember, the Feast is not just a bunch of rules to follow, but they are strategic times that God wants to enjoy His people. My experience while in Jerusalem, Israel at Feast of Tabernacles, on the first night, we had blow the shofars to mark the beginning of Feasts of Tabernacles and the Lord had me sit outside in the Sukkot and began calling people back in the USA and releasing a blessing out of Zion from in the Sukkot over them. The presence of the Lord was so powerful that it was as if I were rising out of my chair off my feet every time I would release the blessing. I was blown away! His Presence was so strong and tangible. I have decided if I'm not in Israel next year at Feast of Tabernacles, I'm going to have a Sukkot and spend time in His presence.

Service of Feast of Tabernacles/Sukkot

As I said before you don't have to build a booth, but your main objective is to celebrate God's goodness. You want to spend time tabernacling (spending time) with the Lord. Studying the word, remembering how God has been good to you and your family and friends. He wants to spend time with us and have a strong relationship with us. Remember:

Exodus 25:8 says, *"And let them make Me a sanctuary, that I may dwell among them.*

Jesus and the disciples celebrated every one of the Feasts. Remember Jesus said in Matthew 5:17, *"Do not think that I came to destroy the Law or the Prophets. I did not come to destroy but to fulfill. He came to fulfill the laws regarding the Feast as well. Many of us in the church have thought Feast were Jewish Customs only, but God has said that these are My Holy Days.*

Leviticus 23:39 - *'Also on the fifteenth day of the seventh month, when you have gathered in the fruit of the land, you shall* **keep the feast of the LORD** *for seven days; on the first day there shall be a sabbath-rest, and on the eighth day a sabbath-rest.*

Judges 21:19 - *Then they said, "In fact, there is a yearly feast of the LORD in Shiloh, which is north of Bethel, on the east side of the highway that goes up from Bethel to Shechem, and south of Lebonah."*

They are to be celebrated throughout all generations by His people.

Exodus 12:42 - *It is a night of solemn observance to the LORD for bringing them out of the land of Egypt. This is that night of the LORD, a solemn observance for all the children of Israel throughout their generations.*

Leviticus 23:21 - *'And you shall proclaim on the same day that it is a holy convocation to you. You shall do no customary work on it. It shall be a statute forever in all your dwellings throughout your generations.*

Leviticus 23:31 - *"You shall do no manner of work; it shall be a statute forever throughout your generations in all your dwellings.*

Numbers 15:23 - *'all that the LORD has commanded you by the hand of Moses, from the day the LORD gave commandment and onward throughout your generations—*

Number 35:29 - *'And these things shall be a statute of judgment to you throughout your generations in all your dwellings.*

There are many more things that could be discussed regarding the other Feasts and God's weekly and monthly calendar for us. Here I just wanted to give us a high-level over view for us to go

185

on our own and ask the Lord to give you sound teaching on His Feast so you can observe them. They are for every one of His sons and daughters regardless of culture. May He bless you as you go forward to discover more about these Feasts and cycles of God's time.

Conclusion

My desire for this book is to bring revelation regarding Abraham having an African wife who bore him six additional sons. There has been much conversation throughout the years regarding Abraham's concubine Hagar who bore him a son named Ishmael. Some have argued that Keturah was a concubine instead of a wife. One of the reasons for this is that some Jews did not want anyone to have the same status as Sarah being the royal wife of Abraham. I know and understand that Sarah was chosen by God to bring forth Isaac, the promised seed, to be included in the lineage of our Lord and Savior Jesus Christ.

This book was not written to argue that point, but it was written to reveal that Abraham had children that had an African mother who are also his seed. Many people have asked me why this information had not been known sooner. This is a very good question because I only realized it by the Holy Spirit and help from several Jewish rabbi's a few years ago. I know I have read through the bible on many occasions and never saw this Scripture. Or maybe I saw it but I didn't have revelation regarding it. The Bible says in Ecclesiastes 3:1, *"To everything there is a season, a time for every purpose under heaven."* I believe that the time and season for this revelation to be revealed is NOW! Ecclesiastes 3:3 says, *"A time to kill, And a time to heal; A time to break down, and a time to build up."*

The African and African-American people have gone through many things for years and years. They have seen the time when they were killed through slavery and other atrocities. And now God wants to completely heal them. They have gone through many years of being broken down. Their families have been broken down, relationships have been broken down, the women have been broken down, the men have been broken down and the children have been broken down. This has happened financially, socially, educationally and spiritually. But the good news is that our great God is saying now it is time to build African-Americans and Hispanics up and to restore. Isaiah 58:12 says, *"Those from among you shall build the old waste places; You shall raise up the foundations of many generations; And you shall be called the Repairer of the Breach, The Restorer of Streets to Dwell In."* Many have misunderstood the purpose of this revelation of Keturah. It is not to say one group is greater than any other group but it is to help restore identity to a group of people. If a person hasn't had their identity stolen it is hard to understand how years and years of not knowing who you are can affect a person's life. I ask that we all pray and asked the Lord what part we should play in helping to restore our African, African-American and Hispanic brothers and sisters to a position of wholeness. As we study Ephesians 2:15, it says having abolished in His flesh the enmity, that is, the law of commandments contained in ordinances, so as to create in Himself **one new man from the two, thus making peace.** I believe in order for God's kingdom to be able to come to the place of peace and walk as the one new man we must all be reconciled to one another.

Appendix 1: Apologies

Christian Organizations Apology

- Southern Baptist Convention (1995) (National Public Radio transcript)
- The Call (7-7-07)
- Presbyterian General Assembly (Oxford UP)
- Heartland Apostolic Prayer Network
- United States Reformation Prayer Network
- House of David
- And many other organizations on many different levels

Federal Government

July 8, 2003, during a trip to Goree Island, Senegal, a former slave port, President George W. Bush acknowledged the continuing legacy of slavery in life in the United States and the need to confront that legacy, when he stated that slavery "was . . . one of the greatest crimes of history."

President Bill Clinton also acknowledged the deep seated problems caused by the continuing legacy of racism against African-Americans that began with slavery.

The United States Senate apologized for slavery on June 11, 2009. (*Washington Post*)

The United States House of Representatives apologized for slavery on July 29, 2009. (*Washington Post*)

The United States House of Representatives apologized for lynchings in 2005. (*Washington Post*)

State Governments

Alabama (2007)
New Jersey (January 3, 2008)
New York (June 2007)
Connecticut (June 5, 2009)
Virginia (2007)
North Carolina (2007)
Maryland (2007)

Florida (March 2008)
States Considering an Apology
Rhode Island
Kansas
Missouri
Nebraska
Arkansas
Delaware
Georgia-Bill revived
Tennessee

Businesses

Aetna (2000) - Apologized for selling policies in the 1850's that reimbursed slave owners for financial losses when their slaves died. Aetna acknowledged that for several years, shortly after its founding in 1853, that the company may have insured the lives of slaves. (*New York Times*)

Brown University (2000) - Rhode Island offered a formal apology for its role in slavery. Brown's endowment came from slave owner's wealth. (*New York Times*)

Wachovia Corp (2005) - Revealed that one bank it acquired had put thousands of slaves to work on a railroad. (*CNN/Money*)

JP Morgan (2005) - Apologized for the role that a subsidiary had played in using 10,000 slaves as collateral and accepting more than 1,000 slaves as payment when owners defaulted on loans. (*CNN/Money*)

Hartford Courant - Apologized for slave trade ads. (*The Providence Journal*, 2000)

Appendix 2: Economics of Slavery

In 2008, the American Humanist Association published an article which argued that if emancipated slaves had been allowed to possess and retain the profits of their labor, their descendants might now control a much larger share of American social and monetary wealth. Not only did the freedmen and freedwomen not receive a share of these profits, but they were stripped of the small amounts of compensation paid to some of them during Reconstruction.

The wealth of the United States, they say, was greatly enhanced by the exploitation of Black slave labor. According to this view, reparations would be valuable primarily as a way of correcting modern economic imbalance. The U.S. Department of Commerce has calculated that in modern U.S. dollars calculated for inflation and interest, slavery generated trillions of dollars for the U.S. economy.

Slavery is fundamentally an economic phenomenon. Throughout history, slavery has existed where it has been economically worthwhile to those in power. The principal example in modern times is the U.S. South. Nearly four million slaves with a market value of close to $4 billion lived in the U.S. just before the Civil War.

Masters enjoyed rates of return on slaves comparable to those on other assets; cotton consumers, insurance companies, and industrial enterprises benefited from slavery as well. Such valuable property required rules to protect it, and the institutional practices surrounding slavery display a sophistication that rivals modern-day law and business.

Appendix 3: African-American Curses
Liberia, West Africa

We found another reason that African -Americans are still cursed is because of what we did to our brothers and sisters in Liberia, West Africa.

The Freed African Slaves did some of the same things that were done to us in slavery to them. They misrepresented the gospel to them and put them in bondage.

We introduced them to the gospel and mixed it with Free Masonry.

Freed Slaves Americanized Liberia, and were called Americo-Liberians.

Freed slaves changed the name of the capital of Liberia from Christoplis (Christ Land) to Monrovia after President James Monroe.

Freed slaves did not want to mix with the Liberians because they thought they were better than them.

We have begun doing reconciliation meetings with the Liberians which is what the African-American Freed Slaves need to do.

I have Liberians that are members of my church who brought this to my attention.

I have taken a team to Liberia to meet with several pastors, government leaders, and business leaders and held reconciliation meetings. The response was overwhelming accepted and many people are continuing to receive the healing and deliverance that's needed to move forward in Christ.

We are going to continue hosting meeting in Liberia, but we are looking to plant churches, open businesses, develop communities and start schools.

There are 10% of people who have, and 90% who have not. We want to create a middle class.

Liberia is the second poorest nation in the world, yet it used to be the second largest producer of rubber in the world.

There are rubber companies that have been there for more than 100 years exploiting the people.

We believe God wants to bring restoration to them and bring restoration to those who have oppressed them.

References

Got Questions Ministries.com
Halley's Bible Handbook, Henry H.
Halley, Zondervan Pub. House, Grand
Rapids, Hamilton, Victor P.(1990), The
Book of Genesis: Chapter 1-17 (Grand
Rapids, MI: Eric Lyons, Eerdmans).
Rabin, Chaim (19740, "The Origin of
the Hebrew word Pileges," Journal of
Jewish Studies, 25:362 by
Apologetics Press
230 Landmark Drive
Montgomery, Alabama 36117
U.S.A.
Phone (334) 2172-8558

Abarim Publications
Holman Bible Dictionary
Fausset's Bible Dictionary
Hitchcock's Bible Dictionary
Wikipedia, Dictionary by Farlex,
Orphan Facts | eHow.com http://www.
ehow.com/about 5404009 orphan.
html#ixzz2DRF6Nhii
Webster College Dictionary

**James W. Goll, Praying for Israel's
Destiny with Chosen Books.**
Chad Taylor
Consuming Fire Revival Network
Email: help@consumingfire.com

Elijah List Publications
310 2nd Ave SE,
Albany, OR 97321

www.elijahlist.com
E-mail: info@elijahlist.net
Phone 1-541-926-3250

Rabbi Curt Landry House of David
Ministries
Dr. Chuck Pierce, Glory of Zion
Ministries, Inc
Dr. Neigel Bigpond, Two Rivers
Ministries
Pastor Tony Cavener, North East
Metro Christian Fellowship
Kim Clement, Kim Clement Center
James W. Goll, Praying for Israel's
Destiny with Chosen Books.
Joseph Ginat, Department of Arab
Affairs, Israel
Apostle Gene Moody, Demonbuster
Website –
Stan and Elizabeth, End-Time
Deliverance Ministry, website (http://
www.demonbuster.com)

All Scriptures are from the New King
James version of the Bible unless
otherwise noted.

For Information about Dr. Venessa
Battle, write to P.O. Box 2156,
Lilburn, Georgia, 30048.